Jewish
Meditations
on the
Meaning of Death

JEWISH
MEDITATIONS
ON THE
MEANING OF DEATH

Chaim Z. Rozwaski

JASON ARONSON INC.
Northvale, New Jersey
London

This book was set in 11 pt. Schneidler by Lind Graphics of Upper Saddle River, New Jersey, and printed by Haddon Craftsmen of Scranton, Pennsylvania.

Library of Congress Cataloging-in-Publication Data

Rozwaski, Chaim Z.
    Jewish meditations on the meaning of death / by Chaim Z. Rozwaski.
      p. cm.
    Includes bibliographical references and index.
    ISBN 1-56821-081-7
    1. Funeral sermons, Jewish. 2. Jewish sermons, American.
3. Homiletical illustrations, Jewish. 4. Consolation (Judaism)
5. Death–Religious aspects–Judaism. 6. Judaism–Doctrines.
I. Title.
BM744.3.R69   1994
296.4′2–dc20

                                                         93-31385

Manufactured in the United States of America. Jason Aronson Inc. offers books and cassettes. For information and catalog write to Jason Aronson Inc., 230 Livingston Street, Northvale, New Jersey 07647.

L'zecher Olam – in loving memory.
I dedicate this book
to the eternal memory
of my loving parents,
David and Basia Rozwaski,
who gave me life.
They were righteous in their life
and pure in their death.
And to my infant brother, Yichiel.
They died the death
of *Kedoshim* – martyrs
during the days of the *Shoah*.
h. y. e. d.

and

My uncle and aunt
Shlomo and Zelda Rozwaski,
who risked their lives to save me
and my sisters, Riva and Mereh,
as well as their own son, Shaul,
from certain death.
They saved our life
during the dark days
of the *Shoah*.

and to

Chief Rabbi Dr. Abraham Kravetz,
himself a survivor,
who was the chief rabbi of Lodz, Poland,
immediately after World War II
and later chief rabbi of Winnipeg, Canada,
where he set me on the course
of my spiritual odyssey.

CONTENTS

CONTENTS

ACKNOWLEDGMENTS

When I began to write this book my intention was to address the immediate needs of people in bereavement. Therefore, I wrote each chapter with the bereaved in mind in the hope of answering their questions and offering them some consolation. Consequently, I purposely omitted footnotes in order to more sharply focus on the goal at hand, which was to comfort people in grief. I believed reference material might distract from that goal.

When Arthur Kurzweil, vice president of Jason Aronson Inc., read the manuscript, he suggested that I should indeed add the footnotes in order to provide references for readers who may want to pursue the subject further, therefore taking into consideration all who might read the book and not only those in mourning.

I gladly accepted his suggestion and have provided footnotes and a bibliography, which I hope will prove to be valuable reference sources for all readers. (When referring to tractates from the Talmud, page numbers indicate whether the source is the Babylonian Talmud [a number followed by "a" or "b"] or the Jerusalem Talmud [a number followed by a colon and another number].)

I want to thank Arthur Kurzweil for his suggestion and encouragingly positive response to my book.

I hope readers will find this book helpful in answering the questions that arise in time of human suffering and healing of the wounds that afflict mankind.

I offer my humble thanks and praise to Him from Whom all healing and comfort come for granting me the privilege of having a share in His work by trying to comfort those who are brokenhearted.

INTRODUCTION

There is a chasidic story about one of the great masters who defined friendship on the basis of a conversation he overheard between two peasants drinking at an inn. As they continued to imbibe and their speech began to slur, one of them good-naturedly slapped his companion on the back and said to him, "Tell me, Ivan, are you my friend?"

"Of course, what a question!" came the quick reply.

"Well then," continued the first one, "if you are my friend, then tell me, what hurts me?"

"How do I know what hurts you?" answered Ivan.

"If you don't know what hurts me," continued the first one, with pain on his face, "how can you be my friend?!"[1]

Indeed, what good is our friendship if we don't know what hurts our friend. And, indeed, when do we need our friend most if not when we hurt the most, which is when we have lost a dear one – a father, a mother, a wife, a husband, a son, a daughter a sister, a brother, or anyone else close to our heart?

---

1. This is the version of the story as I first heard it. Unfortunately I do not recall the name of the storyteller. However, since then I have read the story in the name of Rabbi Moshe Leib of Sassov (the Sassover Rebbe) with a slight variation. See Yehudah Leib Levin, Chasidim Mesaprim – Torah *Va'avodah,* vol. I (Jerusalem: *Mosad Hari'm Levin,* 1968), p. 134.

Another great chasidic master once explained the grief of Aaron the High Priest, who lost his two sons Nadab and Abihu.[2] According to the story in Leviticus, when Aaron found out that his beloved elder sons, who were looked upon as his heirs, died, he "was silent." The Hebrew expression used in this context is "*Vayidom Aharon,*" which could also be translated as "and Aaron was dumbstruck." But, says the chasidic sage, the word "*Vayidom*" sounds very much like the word "*Adom,*" meaning red, and in that case we are subtly reminded that when Aaron heard his sons had died, he turned red; that is, he bled.[3] Indeed both translations are correct. When his sons died, Aaron bled in silence. No words, no shouting, and no crying can express the suffering and the pain, the awesome helplessness of a parent, a wife, a husband, or a child who loses one whom they love. The story of the death of Aaron's sons Nadab and Abihu also tells us that they were buried by their cousins the priests. Nothing is said about the cousins' grief or their compassion for Aaron. Nothing! Not a word. They only buried them. In fact, though, that was all they could have done, because no one can experience, feel, think, and suffer in the same way as the bereaved. All others are merely onlookers.

Like Ivan, we, as well, cannot know what hurts the sufferer. At best we can only help with the burial—with bringing the dead to eternal rest and in doing so, help to bring a little peace of mind to those who survive and be a friend in time of their need and a brother in their hour of suffering.

This is what I hope to do for and be to you—to comfort you in your time of sorrow and befriend you in your hour of need.

---

2. Leviticus 10:1-7.

3. I am indebted to my friend Rabbi Jacob Goldberg of New York, founder and president of the Mourners After-Care Institute, for this interpretation. He told it to me in the name of a chasidic master.

1

Wherever His Words Are, There He Is

You are wondering where your dearly beloved is now. You cannot fathom the meaning of heaven. It is too remote, too vague, and too strange a notion to hold. Perhaps you might find more comfort in knowing that your loved one is not so far away after all.

There is a story that the great chasidic master Rabbi Menachem Mendel of Kotzk tells.[1]

When the great rabbi known as Hayihudi Hakadosh (the Holy Jew) of Przsysucha was dying, everybody was reciting the Psalms on his behalf, but he refused to do so. Rabbi Mendel was standing next to the oven in silence. When he was reproached by Rabbi Bunim for not praying, he did not answer. Later he was told by the same great master, "It's too late for action; the great rabbi of Przsysucha is no longer here," and "he left us the legacy of the fear of heaven; fear of heaven," he continued, "is not something which one leaves in a box. Wherever the rabbi's words are, there is the rabbi." The rabbi was curious to know where that particular place might be and so went looking for it at the place of another great chasidic master. Upon arriving there, he realized it was not the place. However, he recalled being told that the words of the rabbi of Przsysucha remained in the world, and again he went looking for them.

1. Menachem Mendel of Kotzk, *Emeth V'Emunah, Divray Torah, M'rabaynu HaKadosh* (Tel Aviv: Brodi and Katz, 1971), p. 8.

1

He returned to the same rabbi who had told him about it in the first place. Sure enough, he found them there. Furthermore, said the rabbi of Kotzk, the reason he did not reply to the reproach for not reciting the Psalms on behalf of the dying master to begin with was that one cannot think about a second master while the first one is still alive. This was confirmed to him by the same Rabbi Bunim, who said that indeed wherever the words of the master are, there he is too.

It took the rabbi of Kotzk much thought and wandering from place to place to finally realize that one does not disappear from the world when one dies. When we are born, we take up space and time and thought. Life is not like the fire of a match. It does not come into existence with the strike of a hand and disappear with the blow of the mouth without leaving a trace of itself. When one is born, one's birth and life make a difference. And that difference remains even after death. The spiritual dimension remains in this world forever. Each born being contributes its own uniqueness to the world. And that uniqueness remains forever. The uniqueness of the great master of Przsysucha was his fear of heaven. That was his legacy and that was his presence in the world. Wherever there was fear of heaven, there he was too. That truth must apply to all human beings. Wherever any person's creativity took place, there that person is too. The great master of Kotzk learned it from the great master Rabbi Bunim. We learn it from the master of Kotzk.

We want to know where our dearly beloveds are; they are wherever they made an impact on life, wherever their words made an impression. They are not far away. They are near you! They are with you!

2

The Way to Heaven

Many different religions and ways of life are known for their prescriptions for longevity here on earth and the guarantee for eternal life in heaven. Jewish teaching is not so preoccupied with longevity as with the way and the how one ought to live on earth in order to enter heaven. This world, though by all means not to be shunned, is ultimately a preparatory place for entrance into heaven. The way to heaven, however, leads through one's total commitment to make life on this earth good and a better and best of all possible worlds. The means to this end is charity. Acts of charity—the commitment to help others socially, mentally, economically, and in every way possible according to one's means—represent the ultimate way to overcome death itself and secure our place in eternity.

The Talmud relates in the name of Rabbi Judah, who said that God created in the world ten things.[1] Each one of them is stronger than the other. He said, "The rock is hard but iron can split it. Iron is hard but fire can soften it. Fire is hard but water can quench it. Water is strong but the clouds can bear it. The clouds are strong but the wind can disperse them. The wind is strong but the body can bear it. The body is strong but fright can crush it. Fright is strong but wine can banish it. Wine is strong but sleep can work it off. Death is stronger than all but

---

1. *Baba Batra* 10a (Vilna: The Widow and Brothers Romm, 1920).

3

charity saves from death, as it is written, 'Righteousness [charity–tzedakah] delivers from death.' "[2]

This does not mean that charity saves from death and grants longevity. It means that giving charity will save one's soul from destruction in the afterlife and will enable one to be remembered for good in this world, because of one's good deeds by which others were enabled to live.

Our quest, however, is to go beyond mere survival in the world to come. Mankind, by way of sublime efforts and pure pristine existence, has always yearned to behold, if not become part of, the Divine Presence. This has constituted the hope and goal of all who are holy, all philosophers, all seers, and all those of spirit. They tried many different means of attaining this goal. Some have prayed. Others have fasted. Still others practiced asceticism, abstinence, seclusion, confinement to mountains and valleys, and special diets. Many have tried all or some of these in combination. Judaism has never sought to show the way to see and become part of the Divine here on earth. It merely prescribed ways that might help us to behold the Presence of the Divine in the world to come.

Rabbi Dostai, son of Rabbi Jannai, taught the difference between a mortal king and God.[3] He said that if one gives a present to a king, it may or may not be accepted, and even if it is accepted, it is still doubtful if the presenter will be received by the king. God is different. If one gives only a farthing to a beggar, one is treated as if worthy to behold the Divine Presence, for it is written, "I shall behold Thy face in righteousness [tzedakah]. I shall be satisfied when I awake with Thy likeness."[4]

Acts of charity, then, ensure not only eternal life in heaven, but also the privilege of beholding the Divine Presence, a much greater and nobler achievement. We see from this that Rabbi Dostai regarded the virtue of giving charity as an even greater deed than did Rabbi Judah.

Giving charity alone may not be enough. One also has to do it with a sense of humility, piety, and the realization that one should not take for granted one's reward at the hands of God, any more than one may do so at the hands of a mortal king. Thus, when Rabbi Elazar used

---

2. Proverbs 10:2.
3. *Baba Batra*, op. cit.
4. Psalms 17:15.

to give charity, he would immediately say a prayer, because one should pray to God no less than one would pray to a mortal king.[5] Since divine charity leads one to behold the Divine Presence—as it is said, "In righteousness shall I behold Thy face" (that is, when I am giving charity I shall behold Thy face)—one should therefore pray to God at this moment.

Why should the act of charity be so powerful as to bring one face-to-face with God? Because Rabbi Yochanan said,[6] in helping another human being, one becomes a partner of God in His care and protection of His creation, as it is written, "He who has pity on the poor lends to the Lord, and his good deed He will repay unto him."[7] This is a fantastic concept. Imagine God's becoming indebted to us for our helping our fellows! After all, is it not God's responsibility to look after His creatures? Of course it is. That is why God becomes indebted to us for doing His job. Rabbi Yochanan rightly points it out, but he is so taken aback by this very notion, which borders on the presumptuous, that he says,[8] "If it were not written in Scripture, we would never had dared to say it. As it is, it is written, 'the borrower is servant to the lender.' "[9] This applies not only to people but also to God. When we do God's work, God becomes indebted to us no less than we would become indebted to another person for doing our work for us. How great charity is! No wonder those who perform acts of charity may behold the Divine Presence.

Not all people, however, have money to give. What shall such people do? They can do other things. They can give kind words; they can give hard work and time. The greatest thing they can give is to give of themselves, that is, their time and their effort in the pursuit of learning. Students who spend sleepless nights, deny their body the proper rest, and stay up late at night studying also give charity. They give charity with their mind and by denial of their bodily needs. Of them it is written, according to Rabbi Nachman the son of Isaac,[10] "I shall be satisfied when I awake with Thy likeness."[11] The Holy One,

5. *Baba Batra*, op. cit.
6. Ibid.
7. Proverbs 19:17.
8. *Baba Batra*, op. cit.
9. Proverbs 24:6.
10. *Baba Batra*, op. cit.
11. Psalms, op. cit.

blessed be He, feasts upon these scholars, in the world to come, with the resplendence of the Divine Presence.

Charity not only brings us into the Divine Presence but also saves us from the punishment of *geihinom*, as it is written, "Riches profit not in the day of wrath,"[12] which refers to the time of the punishment of *geihinom* and from an unnatural death, as it is written, "but righteousness [*tzedakah*] delivereth from death."[13] So teaches Rabbi Chiyya, son of Abba in the name of Rabbi Yochanan.[14]

Charity has a double power. It has the power to bring one before God and to snatch one from the fires of hell. How magnificent it must be! How simple and how easy it is to avoid oblivion and perdition and to enter heaven and stand in the Presence of God Almighty. One doesn't even have to have money or riches. Just plain learning and devotion to study are enough. One extra hour a week, one more hour a day of less sleep and more study can bring eternal joy. What a small price to pay for such a great gain!

The path to eternity is not through tortuous practices of self-denial, separation from society, or the performance of extraordinary feats. It is through acts of lovingkindness, of caring for our fellows and helping them along their journey in this world, much the way any good fellow traveler who meets another pilgrim in trouble on the road would do. Yes, the way to heaven is that easy. Death only shortens our chances to get there. It can never stop us. Therefore we must never lose any chance to be charitable. It is our ticket to heaven. Use it!

---

12. Proverbs 10:2.
13. Ibid.
14. *Baba Batra,* op. cit. See also the commentary of the Maharsha on the above.

3

In Their Place in Heaven,
No One Else Can Stand

Death takes many forms. We are most accustomed to what is called death from natural causes. Then comes death from unnatural causes, including those that occur under some very traumatic circumstances. One way or another, we manage to cope with such deaths. None of these, however, are treated with pride or celebration. On the contrary, they evoke in us questions and make us feel very bad. However, some deaths bring out in us a feeling of awe, respect, admiration, and pride about those who die. Such are the reactions to the death of people who die heroically. This occurs mainly in times of war, when soldiers and civilians alike are called upon to be self-sacrificing in the name of national interest and a greater common good. People who sacrifice themselves for the sake of others are enshrined in the national memory of their country. They become the heroes of their people. Their death is not so much mourned as it is celebrated from generation to generation and preserved in the books of history.

There are still others, who by their death become not only heroes but saints. These are the men and women who die a martyr's death for a cause, an idea, a concept, or a way of life that they believe in and hold dearly. They die not for others. They die for an abstract concept they have integrated into their own personality and without which they prefer death to life. Such people die under all conditions. It may be in time of war or peace, but so long as their ideas of reality are not accepted, they are ready to die for them. In times of freedom, however, they have no role. They can exist only in times of oppression when countries and nations are ruled by tyrants and dictators who foist their rule by the brutality of force.

There are still others, who choose certain death, not because they are heroes, who want to die in a national cause, or idealists, who prefer death to the compromise of their personal ideals. These are men and women who for the love of other people would rather die themselves and in so doing save others.

One who dies from a natural or unnatural cause has no choice but to die. The soldier who dies a hero's death does so in the heat of battle or in the knowledge of the glory awaiting his memory. The martyr dies in the passion of a cause and the consuming conviction of personal righteousness. Such people have one and the same thing in common: the awareness of themselves and their own importance. The one, however, who chooses to step forward to die in order to save others has no such reason. Why do it, then, if not for a greater love of others than oneself? This one dies because of regarding the life of other people as being more important than one's own, thus showing both love of fellows and personal humility. Such a one really deserves our admiration, respect, and honoring. We ought to remember such a one for a long time, no less than the war hero or the martyr, if not more.

After, the Talmud relates, Joseph the son of Rabbi Joshua fell ill and fainted, he came out from his trance and said to his father, among other things, that he heard in heaven that "No creature can attain the privilege of standing in the place assigned in heaven for the martyrs of the [Roman] government."[1] When the rabbis heard this, they were curious to ascertain who these people were who were held in such lofty esteem. They immediately ruled out the great Rabbi Akiva and his colleagues, who were killed during the same Roman oppressions following the Bar Kochba rebellion in 135 C.E., on the grounds that they merited a unique place in heaven by virtue of their piety and righteousness without having to be martyred.[2] They therefore concluded that this special and extraordinary place in heaven must have been preserved for the martyrs of Lud.[3]

Who are these martyrs?

---

1. *Baba Batra* 10b and *Pesachim* 50a (Vilna: The Widow and Brothers Romm, 1920).
2. Ibid.
3. Ibid.

There were two brothers–Lulianus and Papus–who sacrificed their lives in order to save the people of Lud from being executed by the Romans. According to the accounts of the Talmud, a Roman princess was found dead in the vicinity of the town of Lud. Tarianus, Roman commander of the area, decreed that all the Jews of Lud should be executed unless those who killed the princess were handed over to him. Since the killers were nowhere to be found, the population of Lud was in imminent danger of execution. At that point, the two brothers, in order to save the people of Lud, stepped forward and declared that they had killed the princess. They were executed and the population of Lud was spared.[4] Rashi, commending them on their deed says, "They were absolutely complete righteous people."[5] They gave their lives in order to save the lives of others. They had self-sacrifice, they had love of others, and they were humble, placing the value of the lives of others above their own. They had courage.

What was the background of these two men who are called "absolutely complete righteous people" and into whose presence in heaven no one else may enter?

The Talmud[6] records a conversation between Tarianus and the brothers before they were executed. Said he to them, "If you belong to the nation of Chananiah, Mishal, and Azariah, let your God save you from my hand as He has saved them from the hand of Nevuchadnetzar."

"Chananiah, Mishal, and Azariah," the brothers answered him, "were absolutely complete righteous men and were worthy that a miracle should be performed on their behalf. Furthermore, Nevuchadnetzar was a legitimate king, and therefore he, too, was worthy that a miracle should be performed because of him, but you," they continued, addressing Tarianus, "are a usurper; you are a wicked man and are unworthy that a miracle should be performed on your behalf. We," they added, "deserve to be punished by God in any case because of our misdeeds in general. If you will not kill us, God will kill us by other means. He has many executioners at His disposal. He has many bears and many lions who do His bidding to kill. They can all hurt us and kill

---

4. Rabbeinu Gershom on *Baba Batra,* ibid. See also Rashi's Commentary on same. Regarding the conversation and apparent familiarity, if not friendship, with Rabbi Akiva, see *Berachot* 62b and *Midrash Tanchuma* on *Devarim Ki Tavoh* 2.

5. See Rashi's Commentary on same topic in *Ta'anit* 18b.

6. Ibid.

us. However, the Holy One, blessed be He, has handed us over into your hands now, only in order to avenge our blood upon you by killing you later." The two brothers were killed at the conclusion of their speech. No sooner were they killed, we are told, than messengers arrived from Rome and killed Tarianus.

The tale tells us many things. It tells us that the two brothers had courage. They were not afraid to confront their executioner nor to call him a usurper and a wicked man and warn him that his moment of reckoning at the hands of God would come. It tells us they had honesty. They admitted to not having lived a perfect life. Though they do not tell us what their offenses were, they do imply that they were of a serious nature. They might have been members of the Jewish rebellion against Rome. They also say that, even though they were ready to die in order to save the city, they were innocent of the crime itself. It tells us they had love of their people. What greater proof of that do we need than their willingness to die in order to save others? It tells us also that they had faith in God. They believed that there are both reward and punishment. They believed that God, therefore, holds us accountable for our deeds and that nothing goes unnoticed. They were men who believed in right and wrong, good and bad. They had the integrity and courage to call their executioner by his right name, to admit to their own shortcomings, and to recognize there are people who are worthier than they were. These were their characteristics. No doubt they had many shortcomings as they themselves say. They were not scholars. They were not pious, though they talk of God. They were not God's innocents. They knew the darker side of life. But—they were willing to give their lives for the sake of others. "He who saves one life," we are told, "is to be considered as though he saved the entire world"[7] Lulianus and Papus saved a whole city. They saved many worlds. They earned and deserved an extra special place in heaven, and they got it.

There are in each age and in every place such unsung heroes. Society may not always recognize them, yet they exist, and they die to give life to others. This is especially true in times of war and crisis. We should think of the young men and women who give their lives to save their country, nation, and comrades in arms and should bless them for it. Their memories should live on in our hearts as their souls do in heaven.

---

7. *Sanhedrin* 37a, and also *Baba Batra*, op. cit., 11a. See also the Rambam, *Mishneh Torah* (Vilna: Avraham Tzvi Rozenkrantz and R. Menachem Mendel Schriftzetzer, 1900), *Hilchot Rotze'ach Ushmirat Hanefesh* 1:16.

4

The Lesson of a Funeral

Sometimes something goes wrong at a funeral. All of us can remember instances when a good person's last journey on earth was marred by bad weather, an inappropriate eulogy, an accident on the road to the cemetery, or even a regrettably misguided funeral. Such events only add to the grief and the pain of the survivors. They bring shame to the memory of the departed through no fault of their own. Why do they deserve this and how does one comfort the bereaved?

Rabbi Natan, one of the great sages of the Talmud whose teachings were rooted in the ancient traditions, said, "It is a good sign for the dead when he is punished before his burial. Thus, when one dies and is not properly eulogized or is not properly buried, or if he is dragged along by a wild beast, or if rain falls on his coffin, it is a good sign for him."[1]

All of these events that may befall the deceased are causes for the deceased's humiliation and embarrassment in this world. Rabbi Natan, however, teaches us that they occur in this world to the departed in order to punish misdeeds here in this world, so that the deceased may enter the next world with a clean slate. They serve as an atonement for all sins. They are a sign, indeed, that all will be forgiven and that destiny lies in heaven.

Those who experience mishaps at the funerals of dear ones and friends can take comfort in this lesson of Rabbi Natan.

---

1. *Sanhedrin* 47a.

11

5

The Holy Master

No one wants to die. Everyone struggles to live. It is an intuitive drive.
Similarly, no one wants to see others die either. Instinctively we reach
out to save others, even at the risk of our own life. Yet die we must.
Sooner or later we all die. Why, then, do we struggle to live? Following
is an account of the death of Rabbi Judah the Prince, which might give
us an insight into our struggle both to live and to save others. Let the
Talmud speak for itself.[1]

On the day when Rabbi died, the rabbis declared a public fast and
offered prayers for heavenly mercy. They also said that whoever were
to say that Rabbi was dead would be pierced with a sword.

Rabbi's handmaiden went up on the roof and prayed, "The
heavenly beings want Rabbi to be with them, and the human beings
want Rabbi to be with them. May it be the will of God that the human
beings shall overpower the heavenly beings."[2] However, when she
saw how often he resorted to the toilet (because of his stomach trouble)
and how much he suffered when he removed and put on his *tefilin*
(because he was so weak), she prayed, "May it be the will of God that
the heavenly beings shall overpower the human beings."[3] The rabbis,
however, continually prayed for heavenly mercy on behalf of Rabbi,

---

1. *Ketubot* 104a (Vilna: The Widow and Brothers Romm, 1920).
2. Ibid.
3. Ibid.

and nothing happened to him. She, therefore, took up a clay wine jar to
the roof and threw it down to the ground. When the jar crashed, the
rabbis were startled and, for a moment, ceased praying for heavenly
mercy. At that moment, the soul of Rabbi departed to its eternal rest.
Wanting to know what happened to their beloved master and friend,
the rabbis said to Bar Kapara, one of their colleagues, "Go inside and
investigate how Rabbi is."[4] Bar Kapara went in and when he saw that
Rabbi was dead, he tore his cloak and turned the tear around to his
back. On returning to the rabbis, he said, "The heavenly beings and the
righteous human beings have taken hold of the holy ark (and each side
is pulling it to itself). The heavenly beings have overpowered the
righteous human beings, and the holy ark has been captured."

"Has he gone to his eternal rest?" they asked him.

"You said it, I didn't," he replied.[5]

We are also informed in the Talmud that at the time when Rabbi
passed away, he raised his ten fingers toward heaven and said, "Master
of the universe, it is revealed and known to you that I have labored in
the study of the Torah with my ten fingers and that I did not enjoy any
worldly benefits, even with my little finger. May it be Your will that
there be peace in my final resting place."

Whereupon, a heavenly voice proclaimed, "He shall enter into
peace; they shall rest on their beds."

At that point, we are told the rabbis raised a technical question,
"Does not the context require the usage of the singular pronoun
'*mishkavcha*' – on your bed – instead of the plural '*mishkevotam*' – on their
beds?"[6]

The Maharsha[7] raises a number of questions about this account of
the death of Rabbi Judah the Prince. He also provides us with the
answers, which are most illuminating.

These are the questions that trouble him.

1. Why did the rabbis decree that anyone who says that Rabbi died
   shall be pierced by a sword? Indeed, at the end, they themselves
   asked, "Did his soul find its eternal rest?"

---

4. Ibid.
5. Ibid.
6. Ibid.
7. See the Commentary of the Maharsha (Moreinu Hagaon Rabbi Shmuel Eliezer
Halevi Edels).

2. What is the meaning of the statement concerning the heavenly beings desiring Rabbi?

3. What is the meaning of the fact that the vessel the handmaiden threw down was a clay wine jar?

4. What is the meaning of the reference to the holy ark and its being captured, rather than the Torah, which is in the ark itself?

5. What is the meaning of Rabbi's lifting up his ten fingers? Indeed, why does he not say the same thing about his entire body, namely, that he did not benefit from this world, even with his smallest limb?

6. Why does the Talmud question the usage of the plural of the word "bed" and not the plural of the word "rest," which is also stated in the same sentence?

The Maharsha responds by postulating the following.

It is understood that we are created as a composite of both the soul, which comes from the upper, spiritual world, and the body, which is derived from the lower, material world. Consequently, we have two faculties. One is the faculty of intellect, derived from the soul. The other is the ability to act, derived from the body. Because Rabbi achieved absolute intellectual perfection in the study of the Torah and in the performance of its precepts, as it is said, "On the day when Rabbi Judah died the concept of holiness was negated,"[8] that is, he was reduced to the level of a mortal, and furthermore, "the concepts of humility and fear of heaven were negated,"[9] *he was* therefore, based on his Torah wisdom and his performance of good deeds, *worthy to live forever and ever.* Indeed, that is why he was called "Our Holy Master."[10] Therefore the rabbis decreed that whoever were to say that he was dead should be pierced by a sword, because such a statement would negate his greatness. In addition to these reasons, there is also the fact that all his life he suffered pain on behalf of the people of his time, as we have been taught, "All the years that Rabbi suffered the world did not lack rain."[11] They could not accept the fact that now they would begin to experience drought and suffering again. Therefore they

---

8. *Ketubot* 103b.

9. *Sotah* 49a (Vilna: The Widow and Brothers Romm, 1920).

10. *Ketubot* 103b. See also the Commentary by *Tosefot.*

11. *Baba Metzia* 84b.

said, "Whoever will say that he died shall be pierced by a sword,"[12] for he had indeed protected the people of his lifetime.

The matter of the prayer by the handmaiden meant the following. Her reference to the heavenly beings means that the mere fact that Rabbi Judah's soul was immortal made it already part of the heavenly beings even while on earth. Indeed, he would have achieved maximum perfection of his rational faculties in heaven. The human beings (that is, the righteous people) who dwell on earth, however, wanted Rabbi to achieve absolute perfection through the performance of the bodily precepts (not the intellectual ones) here in this world; therefore, they wanted him to continue to live eternally in body and soul. When, however, the handmaiden saw him suffer very much and that it was impossible for him to attain perfection of his bodily faculties as illustrated by the fact that he had difficulty with the *tefilin*, she consequently said, "May it be God's will that the heavenly beings shall overpower the human beings."[13] Because the rabbis kept on praying for God's mercy and thus kept his soul from departing, however, she took a wine jug and broke it in order to distract them. The fact that the jug was from clay teaches us that just as a clay vessel, once it is broken, is dead, a human body, too, once it is broken and in pain, is dead. One cannot achieve bodily perfection (that is, the perfect performance of all the precepts incumbent upon the human body to handle, for example, *tefilin*) when one's body is no longer functioning. The rabbis realized this when the jug was broken. They therefore kept quiet, and Rabbi's soul found its eternal rest.

Bar Kapara tore his cloak and turned it to the back in order not to tell the rabbis directly that Rabbi was dead. However, in doing it this way, he merely gave them a clue. He used the expression "the heavenly beings"[14] wisely. He followed a precedent. He did it by following the teaching of the verse "There is one who speaks like the piercing of a sword, but the tongue of the wise is healing"[15] (Bar Kapara used wisdom in bringing them the sad news and thus avoided their decree).

Now the reason why Bar Kapara states that the heavenly beings and the human beings are fighting over the ark and not the Torah itself,

---

12. Maharsha on *Ketubot* 104a. See also the Maharsha on *Baba Metzia* 84b.
13. *Ketubot* 104a.
14. Ibid.
15. Proverbs 12:18.

which is in the ark, is this. The Torah symbolizes the human soul. The ark symbolizes the human body. Just as the Torah is eternal, so also is the human soul. Just as the ark is destructible, so also is the human body. Rabbi Bar Kapara thus tells us that Rabbi Judah's body was destroyed by death, but his soul was not. A soul lives on forever.[16]

The reason why Rabbi raised his ten fingers when he died is this. At the time of his death, Rabbi lacked only the perfection of his deeds, which are performed by the body. His mind, which is in the power of the soul, was perfect. It will be strengthened even more in the world to come. Therefore, we are told only of the perfection of his physical deeds, which are symbolized by the fingers as the instruments of man's bodily activities. The phrase "have labored with my ten fingers"[17] means therefore, "I have labored in fulfilling the precepts of the Torah," and the phrase "and I have not enjoyed the worldly benefits even with my little finger" means that all his life and all his actions were dedicated to the service of God.[18] Consequently, he prayed, "May it be Thy will that there be peace in my last resting place," that is, "for my body in the grave."[19] It is in response to that request that the heavenly voice said, "He shall enter in peace, they shall rest on their beds"[20] (in the plural). The word *yanuchu* (they shall rest) is used in the plural because it refers to the resting of the body in the grave and the resting of the soul in the world to come, where it will achieve absolute perfection. However, the usage of the word "*mishkevotam*" (their beds) is inappropriate in the plural, for it cannot refer to the soul (as well as the body), as a bed does not apply to the soul. Therefore it is interpreted as referring not to Rabbi but to the souls of the righteous who (rose up from their places) and went out to greet Rabbi. It tells us that their bodies, too, will rest in peace on their beds in their graves. There was no need, however, to plead on behalf of the perfection of the souls of the other righteous people. They will certainly find perfection because of their own merits in the world to come.[21]

We can now draw some conclusions from this account and interpretation of the lesson of the death of Rabbi.

---

16. Maharsha on *Ketubot* 104a.
17. *Ketubot* 104a.
18. Maharsha, op. cit.
19. Ibid.
20. Isaiah 57:2.
21. Maharsha, *Ketubot* 104a.

1. People naturally want to save the lives of their leaders, masters, and friends. They will do anything in their power to do so. They will pray and ask for mercy. They will even defy heaven. The rabbis did both in order to save their beloved Rabbi. However, this is not all. People also have difficulty in accepting the death of those they love and revere. They will go to all lengths to deny the death of their loved one. Thus the rabbis threatened with death anyone who announced that Rabbi died, so Bar Kapara had to use his wit and wisdom to inform them subtly but correctly of it. The denial of death and the clinging to those we love are part of human nature. They are, however, of no avail. Death does not stop.

2. Nobody can live forever. Rabbi, the man who attained the level of being called The Holy One, also had to die. No matter what heights the mind may attain and no matter how much good one does with one's body in this world, no one can live forever. When our body begins to fail us, our spirit will leave us too. When Rabbi's body could function no longer, his life could not go on any longer. Even when his friends wanted to hold on to him, it was of no avail. Rabbi's hand-maiden realized that and so she broke the jar in order to divert the attention of the rabbis from prayer in order to allow Rabbi to go in dignity to his eternal rest in heaven.

3. There is a constant conflict between the body and the soul. In our bodily existence we want to continue living in this world forever. In our spiritual existence we yearn to return to our Divine Source. No matter how much we do, how much we deny our bodily pleasures and emphasize our spiritual and intellectual life, no matter how much we bend our body to do the bidding of our mind by discharging all of God's commandments, the time comes when our body begins to disintegrate, when we must die, and when our soul must return to heaven. That is what Rabbi meant when he said, raising his ten fingers to heaven, that he did not benefit from this world even to the extent of his little finger, because he had devoted his entire being to the service of God. Yet, at the end, he had to die. The only request he had was to rest in peace in the grave.

4. There comes a time when one must resign oneself to death and even pray for it. This is when life loses all dignity and the body its strength and ability to function properly and suffering becomes a steady part of life. This is what happened to Rabbi. His body could function no longer. While the rabbis prayed for him to live because

they could not see life without him, and because they wanted him to live forever, the handmaiden knew better. She saw Rabbi as a broken jar. He could not be cured any more than a broken jar could be made whole again. She therefore prayed for his death so that his suffering should come to an end. Indeed, one of the great masters, Rabbi Nisim Gerondi derives from this event the law that "there are times when it is proper to pray for Divine mercy for a sick person to die, as in a case when one is very sick, suffers much pain, and has no hope of recovery."[22] Even though such a prayer is regarded as an inferior form of prayer than a prayer for recovery, which is a superior one, nevertheless, it too is a prayer that must at times be recited for the benefit of the sick, namely, for release from pain.

We may also conclude from this that life without hope and dignity is not worth living. It is better to offer up one's soul to the Maker than to live a life of suffering, pain, and helplessness. Bodily, life must be lived with the body. When the body no longer functions it is better to surrender it to the grave in peace and return with the soul to heaven.

5. What is the purpose of life? Rabbi Judah the Prince exemplifies what one should strive to be and what one should strive to do. We learn from this account of him and especially the testimonials to his name, which the Maharsha brings, that he had spent his entire life trying to fulfill the commandments and to study the Torah. He served the welfare of his fellow human beings. He used his body to practice the laws and to do good things for others. He used his mind to acquire understanding and wisdom in order to serve both his fellows and God the better. When his time came to die, he asked only for peace in the grave. How little he was content with! From another source, we also know that he made other requests, but all of them had to do with the welfare, interest, and lifestyle of others: his children, his wife, his household, his academy, and his people in the towns and cities. For himself he asked for nothing except to be buried in a perforated coffin and a simple shroud. Imagine, this great man, all he wanted out of his life was peace in his grave (see chapter 8).

There is a story by a great Yiddish writer, Y. L. Peretz, called

---

22. Rabbi Nisim Gerondi (Ran) on *Nedarim* 40a (Vilna: The Widow and Brothers Romm, 1920). See also the Maharsha, who takes exception to this interpretation.

"Bontche Shvaig—Bontche the Silent One."[23] It is about a man who was a water carrier and who worked day in, day out, from early dawn until late at night, carrying buckets of water from the town well to the townspeople. He did it in the infernal heat of the summers and the freezing cold of the winters. Many a time he would fall on the icy and hilly streets and cut himself. His blood would gush, but he kept silent. He never complained. When night fell, he barely had anything to eat. He didn't complain about that either. When children and even adults made fun of him and mocked him in the streets, he would keep quiet. He took the pain and the insults from the weather as from the people. Each day he would rise early and recite his prayers, thanking God for all His blessings, and at night he would recite his prayers again. One day he fell ill and died. When this happened, the angels came running to God, telling Him that his faithful servant Bontche had died. How shall they greet him, they asked of God. "Bring him before my Heavenly Throne," God said. "I want to welcome him in person." The word went out and preparations were made in heaven for a Divine Reception for God's servant Bontche.

All the heavenly beings were full of excitement. The angels wer running back and forth, trying to get ready for the special moment Never before had God welcomed anyone in person. Never before ha such a thing been heard of. Finally, the great moment arrived. Th reception was ready. God was sitting on His Heavenly Throne, su rounded by his angels—Michael, Gabriel, and all the others—who wei all dressed up for this special occasion. Bontche arrived. Everybod rose, even God. "Welcome, my son Bontche," God announced. "W are waiting to greet you, receive you, and reward you for the exen plary life you have led. Ask, ask anything you want and it shall l granted to you!"

Bontche was stunned! He was overwhelmed. He was shakin Finally, he muttered, "You mean it? I can really have whatevei want?" "Yes, go ahead and ask!" said God.

Bontche waited a second. He thought a little longer. At last said, "May I have a bread roll and a glass of hot milk?"

---

23. Yehuda Leib Peretz, *Yehuda Leib Peretz*, ed. A. S. Rappoport (Freeport, NY: Boc for Library Press, 1971): Y. L. Peretz, *Shriften, Naye Fergreserte Oiflage. Zeveiter Band* (N York: Hebrew Publishing Co.).

That was all that Bontche asked for. In his lifetime he could conceive only of a bread roll and a glass of hot milk as the supreme luxury. And when he died, he could finally have it.

Rabbi was quite different. In his lifetime he was the Prince of the Nation. He could have had everything he desired, but he didn't even enjoy the worldly benefits with his little finger. All he wanted at the end of his journey was to have peace in his last resting place.

Some people want only a piece of bread out of life; others just a peaceful resting place.

6. The most puzzling thing about the description of the last day of Rabbi's life is that, except for statements that he did not enjoy the worldly benefits and was incontinent and was putting on and taking off his *tefilin* with difficulty, we hear very little from him. All we are told is what the others said and did. We are told very little about Rabbi himself. Here we have a scene where a great man is dying and everybody is running around him, but he is busy with the *tefilin*. He is silent. When he finally speaks, all he says is that he wants to rest in peace in his grave. He is otherwise silent!

How sad, how painful, how pregnant with wisdom such silence must be. Rabbi is dying and saying nothing. He is not sad, he is not crying, he is not complaining. He is too busy with the *tefilin*. Everybody else is crying, praying, and even denying his impending death, as well as passing decrees and proclaiming fasts, but he, he is silent! Rabbi was not a passive person. He lived an active, dynamic, creative, and even at times turbulent life, full of public worries, concern, strife, and intellectual confrontation and challenge. He was not a man of silence. Yet at his death, he kept silent. Why? Because when the moment of truth arrives, words are of no avail. When one is about to approach the Heavenly Throne, one has no words. In the presence of God, all creation is silent.[24]

As he was dying, Rabbi knew what was happening. He had led a life of holiness and now he was ready to join all who are holy. He knew that God had brought him into the world and God was about to take him out of the world. The important thing while being in the

---

24. Habakkuk 2:20: "The Lord is in His Holy Temple; let all the earth keep silence before Him"; Zephaniah 1:7: "Hold thy peace at the presence of the Lord"; Zechariah 2:17: "Be silent, all flesh, before the Lord."

world is to be doing God's bidding and while going to heaven, it is still important to continue to do God's bidding. Rabbi did both. That is why he had the *tefilin* on him. As long as his body allowed him, he had the *tefilin*, which symbolizes God's words, upon him, and when his body failed him, he departed with God's words still on him. The *tefilin* were his link with God in this world and their message carried on the parchment inside them – "Hear, O Israel, the Lord your God, the Lord is One. You shall love the Lord your God, with all your heart, with all your soul, and with all your might"[25] – was with him as he went to heaven. He lived and he died by those words. He need not have said anything else. The *tefilin* spoke for him. He was ready to enter heaven in peace.

---

25. Deuteronomy 6:4.

6

Remember with Joy

When death strikes at our door, we often ask, "Why? Why me? Why us?" These are spontaneous reactions to sudden shock and loss. They are often followed up by a series of other questions such as, "Where is God? Does He care? Does He know?"

I have often had to listen to grief-stricken wives, bereaved husbands, heartbroken parents, and sorrowful children who strike out at God with tears in their eyes, pain in their heart, and trembling in their voice. It is not unnatural in times of sorrow to express one's total helplessness and frustration by turning against God. Who else? Hasn't the death of our dear one just taught us already that we are helpless? It is the time when we recognize the most deeply how vulnerable we are. Therefore, it becomes the time when we need God the most. We therefore turn to God, the All-Powerful, Who could, but didn't, help. Consequently, we are caught on the horns of a paradoxical dilemma. Our need for God's help is the strongest and His response is the weakest. This is when some of us become consciously or subconsciously aware of such thoughts and feelings as, "We are helpless to save life" and "Only God could have saved our dear one; why didn't He?" In the heat of our pain we turned for help to God. In the sorrow of our disappointment, when He, the All-Powerful, didn't respond and didn't help, we turn in anger away from or against Him. Some of us begin to doubt God and to think in the heat of our anguish that perhaps

God doesn't care or doesn't want to help and, worst of all, may not even be aware of what is happening to us altogether.

The consequences of such reactions to the death of a dear one are many. They are found particularly among younger people, such as on the part of a young husband who loses his wife in the prime of her life, a wife whose husband dies when they had just started living, parents whose daughter or son has died in the spring of youth, and children who are left without a parent. People in such circumstances become bitter and hostile toward God, rejecting Him, perhaps for the rest of their life, unfortunately, to their own detriment. They are haunted throughout life by their own question, "If God knows, why doesn't He care, and if He cares, why didn't He help?" If He didn't help, He neither cares nor knows, they conclude. Unfortunately, neither life nor God nor the relationship between us and God is that simple. Ultimately, God reveals His knowledge, His care, and His help. Unfortunately, when we realize that God cares and helps and knows, it is often too late to correct our mistakes.

There is a beautiful story the rabbis tell that explains God's knowledge of us and how we relate to one another. The rabbis assert, "In the world to come, God will reprove everyone for deeds in this world."[1] In making that assertion, the rabbis are concerned with the question of how God will know what each one of us does in this world. They respond by illustrating their answer with the following story.

The relationship between God and people, they say, is similar to this. There was a man who was married to the daughter of a king. The man would come every morning to greet the king. The king would promptly say to him, "You have done such and such in your house; you have been angry in such and such a way; you have beaten your servant in this and that manner." The son-in-law would return to his palace and ask those who lived with him, "Who told the king what I did? How does he know it?" They answered him, "Fool, you are married to the king's daughter and you are asking, 'How does he know?' His daughter is telling him!"[2]

Thus it is also true of us. We do whatever our heart desires and our soul tells everything to the Holy One, praised be He. He then judges us,

---

1. *Pesikta Rabbati* 8:2.
2. Ibid.

saying, "You have done this and this and that and that," for it is written, "The lamp of the Lord is the soul of man, searching all the inward parts."[3]

Indeed, we may not realize it, but God is linked to us through the soul, which is the Divine Gift to us all. This soul, which is of God, makes us what we are and differentiates us from all other creatures. The soul knows everything we do. It is like a lamp by which God looks into and sees our innermost thoughts and feelings. Nothing is hidden from Him. While we are alive, the soul may be our conscience, our spiritual uniqueness, and the mover of all our deeds, but when it returns from our body to its heavenly abode, it brings back with it a full report of all our actions here on earth. It does this faithfully, and God therefore knows clearly everything we did.

When life departs from the body of our dear one, whom we have to lay to rest, the time of that dear one's retribution begins. We who remain behind, too busy dealing with our own grief, cannot fathom what is happening to the soul of our departed. We only miss him or her. We only want him or her back with us. We can only worry about what will happen to us; how will we continue to live without him or her? We forget that it was a Power much greater than we that brought us together in the first place. That very Power has now taken us apart. It was a Force stronger than both of us that kept us together. It will be the same Force that will keep us in life. He Who provided for and protected us in the past will protect and provide for us in the future. He Who is judging for good and with compassion the soul of our dear departed, who stands before Him in absolute truth, will also care for us with mercy and love.

At one time in life, we and our dear one were joined together because it was time that we should be united in this world. We are now apart because the time has come for us to separate in this physical world. Just as the soul comes into and leaves the body, so too, people – husbands and wives, parents and children, brothers and sisters, lovers and friends, relatives and neighbors – are at the right time in life brought together and at the proper time taken apart. He Who knows when to unite us also knows when to separate us. In His own good time He shall unite us again.

Until then, let us cherish the good times, the beautiful memories,

---

3. Proverbs 20:27.

the wonderful things we did together, both when times were bad and when times were good.

There is a time to mourn and a time to laugh, isn't there?

There is a time to be brought together and a time to be taken apart, isn't there?

There is a time to do things and a time to remember them, isn't there?

You had your time to do. Now is the time to remember.

Remember with joy!

7

Bound in the Bond of Eternal Life

When death strikes we are faced with a sudden awareness of our own being. It is paradoxical how through the loss of someone else we become conscious of ourselves as though our own existence had been taken for granted up to this point, and only when we begin to feel the loss of one who is no longer here, do we begin to feel our own existence. This is what mourning, grief, and bereavement are all about. They express our loss, our separation, our loneliness, and our fear of being alone without the support, companionship, friendship, and love of the one who is now dead. Therefore, we reach out to one another in time of mourning in order to comfort, console, and help those who are in grief. However, death is also a moment when we should worry about what is happening to the departed. Does life after death really come to a total end? Is our dear one's existence extinguished once the body is buried? Does death bring an end to everything, including our need to worry about what lies in store for the dead, who have in their death crossed the threshold between this world of ours and entered into the unknown world of the future and eternity? If the answer is yes, then indeed we should glibly conclude with the trite words so often heard on the lips of those who come to pay their last respects, "Well, his worries are now over," then turn our back on the dead and face the task of helping only the survivors. However, if our answer is no, death does not end all and there is a life after death, then indeed we must turn to the departed in order to find out what lies in store for him or her after the journey on this earth has ended. Indeed, we might find comfort in knowing what awaits the dead in the future world. This knowledge might even bring hope and comfort to all of us who are still left in this world and certainly to the mourners who need–especially now, in their loneliness–reassurance that those whom they mourn are doing well, thus inspiring them to rejoin the stream of life in order to make this a better place for all.

The need to comfort the bereaved is an old one. It might, therefore, be helpful for us today to learn how, over the ages, our forebears understood the meaning of life after death, for they, too, needed to be comforted in time of death and sorrow no less than we do, and they also wanted to know what happens after death.

Said Rabbi Elazar,[1] we are told in the Talmud, "When a righteous man departs this world, three groups of ministering angels come out to greet him. One of them says to him, 'Come into peace'[2]; another one says, 'He who walketh in his uprightness'[3]; and the third one says, 'He shall enter into peace, they shall rest upon their beds.' "[4] What does this statement mean?

The three groups of ministering angels are each quoting a part of Isaiah 57:2, which reads in its entirety, "He enters into peace, they shall rest in their beds, each one that walks in his uprightness."[5]

The meaning of the verse is that God says it is better for the upright persons to die ahead of their time than to live to see the trouble that is to befall the world, and furthermore when they die, they will be received into peace eternal. Such upright people will rest in peace in their bed in heaven forever. They will not be disturbed in their grave, because they have led an upright life. Indeed, it would not be proper that they should not be resting in peace in heaven without any disturbance to their mortal remains in the grave. Thus righteous persons upon death are greeted by peace. They find eternal tranquillity in the grave for their mortal remains, and for their soul in heaven,

---

1. *Ketubot* 104a.
2. Isaiah 57:2.
3. Ibid.
4. Ibid.
5. Ibid. The Hebrew word *yanuchu* (rest) is in the plural, whereas the word *yavo* (He shall come) is in the singular. This contradiction between the singular and plural forms the basis for additional interpretations of the meaning of the verse.

because they walked uprightly here on earth during their lifetime.[6]

The rabbis in the story alter this passage of Isaiah and interpret it this way: When the righteous die, they are greeted in heaven by one group of ministering angels, who welcome them in peace by saying, "Come into peace," which is the nature of heaven itself. Another group proclaims the departed's merits and the reason why they are welcomed into peace, namely, because they were among those who "walked in uprightness" here on earth. A third group of angels proclaims the remains will also rest in peace here on earth when they say "they rest in their beds."[7]

There is another interpretation, however, which maintains that this is a reference to the souls of the righteous people who rise up and go out to greet the arrival of a righteous one into heaven and after whose arrival, we are told, return to rest in peace in their beds. That is why the second clause of the verse is in the plural.[8]

The three groups of ministering angels also represent three different parts of heaven: the uppermost, the middle, and the lower levels. The group of ministering angels that proclaims, "Enter into peace," represents the uppermost level of heaven. This is where supreme peace reigns in the Heavenly Court. There, the soul of the righteous is bound up in the bond of eternal life. The group of angels that proclaims, "They that walk in their uprightness," represents the middle level of heaven. That is, the place where the righteous goes because of uprightness in negating the fortunes of nature is the place where our spirit (*ruach*, not *neshamah*–soul) enters. The third group of ministering angels, which says, "They rest in their beds," represents the lower world, in which the body is buried.[9]

It now becomes clear that when the righteous die, they are not only welcomed into Heaven by the ministering angels and the righteous people who went there before but also welcomed into different states of eternity. They are assured that their earthly remains will not be disturbed, their spirit will find rest in the afterlife, and their soul will be welcomed into eternal peace. In addition to that, we are told that

---

6. Rashi, Commentary on both *Ketubot* 104a and Isaiah 57:2. See also the Malbim on Isaiah 57:2.

7. Maharsha on *Ketubot* 104a.

8. Ibid.

9. Ibid.

death will save them from seeing the troubles that might befall the world and thus their own suffering and pain.

These are indeed comforting and reassuring thoughts. Life after death need not be one of hellfire and brimstone. It can be blissful, beautiful, and smooth for eternity. Those who know that they have lived a life to the best of their ability can anticipate a future of peace. Those who know how nice, good, and upright their dearly departed were, can rest assured that they, too, are in heaven now.

May you find comfort in these thoughts.

8

The Way to Die

Some people live and die and nobody is any the wiser for that. Some people make a name for themselves by the way they die. Others do so by the way they live. Still others spend a lifetime for the sake of their fellows, and when they die, they also make sure that others will benefit from them. Indeed, people like that live and die to teach and help others. Such a man was Rabbi Judah the Prince.

The rabbis teach us that when Rabbi Judah was about to die, he called for his sons. When they came to him, he said to them:

1. "Be sure to carefully protect your mother's honor."
2. "The [Sabbath] light should be kept burning in its usual place."
3. "The table should continue to be laid in its usual place."
4. "The bed should continue to be spread in its usual place."
5. "Yosef of Haifa and Shimon of Efrat attended to me when I was alive. They should also attend to me at my death."[1]

It is also said that in addition, he said to his colleagues the rabbis:

6. "You should not eulogize me in the smaller towns."
7. "Reassemble the college after thirty days."
8. "My son Simeon is wise, my son Gamliel is the *nasi* [shall be the

---

1. *Ketubot* 103a.

Prince] and Chaninah bar Chama shall preside [at the college]."[2]

9. "My wife shall not be moved from my house."[3] Rabbi Chizkiah adds two more requests that Rabbi Judah made before he died. According to him, he also said,

10. "Do not dress me in too many garments," and

11. "My casket should be perforated at the bottom."[4]

Now what do these eleven requests mean? If we look at them carefully we shall note that they deal with three distinct areas of life and human relations: family, public conduct, and faith.

The instructions that Rabbi Judah left concerning family life, in terms of the relationship between the survivors and their departed father and between themselves, are those that say, "honor your mother, do not move my wife from her house, and keep the Sabbath candle and set the table and my bed in the same place." In requesting these of his heirs, Rabbi Judah wanted to make sure that they would carry on the family traditions and the teachings of their father as symbolized by the Sabbath and the preparation of the household for that occasion, for the Sabbath is the culmination of all of the six days of work, which lead to the day of rest and, in so doing, to the affirmation of all of the teachings of the Torah and the sages. As long as his heirs kept the Sabbath, Rabbi Judah was assured that they would keep all the other rituals as well. However, that did not mean that they would also automatically respect his wife, the widow, and therefore he made a special request for that. This also teaches us that a husband should make the proper provisions for his wife. He should not take it for granted that his children will automatically be nice to her. Family relations are unpredictable. Rabbi Judah made sure that his wife was taken care of and that her social place would not be changed with his death.[5]

The rabbis also say that the reason he requested that the candle, the table, and the bed should all be in their usual place was that he was granted permission to visit, in spirit, his earthly abode every Friday night. That is how great he was. However, one Friday night, a

---

2. Ibid. 103a and 103b.

3. *Bereishit Rabbah (Parshah Vayechi)* 96:5. See also *Midrash Tanchuma* on *Vayechi* 3.

4. *Talmud Yerushalmi, Ketubot* (Jerusalem: *Machon Lehotza'at Sefarim*); Hachatam Sofer, zt"l, 1962; *Hanosei et Ha'ishah, halachah gimel.*

5. *Ketubot* 103a.

neighbor visited the house. He spoke very loudly. When the maid told him to lower his voice because Rabbi Judah was sitting at the table, Rabbi Judah thereupon realized that the man would tell everybody that he was coming home for the Sabbath, and everybody in turn would think that other saintly departeds were not as great as he was and therefore were not granted the privilege of returning for the Sabbath to their home. In order not to create that impression he never returned again to his home.[6]

This, too, teaches us not only about the humility of Rabbi Judah but also that things that may be done in the privacy of one's family should be avoided in public. A family is a special place. Within the confines of a family one may take certain privileges that one cannot take in public. Therefore, families have to be discreet about each other. This applies to good things. How much more so does it apply when we deal with bad things.

There is also another moral to the story. One may enjoy certain advantages in life, provided these are not done at the expense of others. As long as nobody knew about Rabbi Judah's visits, no one was hurt. But the moment it became public, the other sages might have felt slighted. Rabbi Judah therefore could no longer enjoy his visits.[7]

Rabbi Judah's instructions dealing with public conduct and relations are concerned with who should attend to him after his death, the reopening of the colleges, where he should be eulogized, and the designation of who should lead the community after his death. According to the various interpreters of these requests, Rabbi Judah made them in order not to impose undue embarrassment, hardship, and quarrels.[8] It would have been grossly offensive to Yosef of Haifa and Shimon of Efrat if after long and devoted service to their master, they had not been allowed to attend to him after his death.[9] Indeed, it is taught that "he who embarrasses his fellow man in public does not have a portion in the world to come."[10] There is no greater social sin

---

6. Rashi on *Ketubot* 103a.

7. *Ketubot* 103a, because people would have said that they were less worthy than he was.

8. *Ketubot* 103a. The villages, towns, and cities would argue with each other over which one of them should have the honor of eulogizing Rabbi first. (See also Rashi on the same.)

9. Ibid.

10. *Baba Metzia* 58b–59a and *Avot* 3:15, as well as *Midrash Rabbah* on Genesis 1:15.

than to disgrace and humiliate one's fellow human being in public. In his last hours, Rabbi Judah made sure this would not happen to his faithful attendants.

There is also another explanation of this event. According to the records, Yosef of Haifa and Shimon of Efrat died before Rabbi Judah, their master. Rabbi Judah, knowing of this, wanted to make sure that no one should say they died in order that they should be denied the privilege of attending to the last rites of their master because they were unworthy thereof due to a flaw in their personalities or some misdeeds. He therefore proclaimed that they would attend to him in the world to come, even as they attended to him in this world, because they are, indeed, fine and worthy people who deserve to continue to be in his presence and thus also in the presence of other saintly persons.[11] What a beautiful testament to one's attendants. Rabbi Judah teaches us that we must show public appreciation, praise, and respect to those who work for us and not merely avoid offending them.

In requesting that the academies reopen after thirty days, Rabbi Judah showed a sense of humility, public concern, and appreciation of the virtue of the pursuit of knowledge. He said that the academies should reopen in order not to give the impression that he is greater than Moses, for whom the people mourned also thirty days.[12] He also showed that public leaders, regardless of how much they are beloved, should not disrupt the routine conduct of life by interfering with the daily activities of society. However, even though we are told the public continued to mourn him for the entire year, they did so not because he asked them to but because they had a need to express their sorrow and loss at his death, in spite of his request.[13] Nevertheless, Rabbi Judah felt that they should continue with the regular study program after thirty days so that learning would not be unduly interrupted.[14] Indeed, it is to be expected of him that he–who went out of his way and who is responsible for the preservation of the Oral Torah, which was threat-

---

11. Ibid., particularly Rashi's and the Maharsha's Commentaries on *Ketubot* 103a.

12. *Ketubot* 103b and Deuteronomy 34:8, "And the children of Israel wept for Moses in the plains of Moab thirty days; and then were ended the days of weeping and mourning for Moses." See Maimonides' *Mishneh Torah, Hilchot Aveilut* 13:10.

13. *Ketubot* 103a. Rashi, ibid.

14. Rashi on *Ketubot* 103b comments on *vehoshivu yeshivah* and return to the *yeshivot*–to the study of the Torah. After thirty days, he adds –*Meyad* (immediately)– and you should not engage in eulogizing beyond it.

ened with extinction due to the forced closing of the schools,[15] by writing of the *Mishnah*, even though it meant he had to reinterpret the injunction against writing down that which was to be transmitted orally–should also insist that his own death not be the cause of the obliteration of the Torah through lack of study.

He also wished that his death should not impose hardship and create arguments among the people. That is why he requested that no eulogies be made for him in the smaller towns, because it would lead to argument among the town dwellers about the venue of the mourning service and impose hardship on the people, who would have to go to the next town or even farther away in order to participate in the memorial service. Better not to have any such services at all than to put the people in a position whereby they would have to argue with each other and suffer hardship.[16] Love of the people must supersede love of one's own honor. That is a great lesson from a great man.

Rabbi Judah was also mindful of the vacuum in the leadership of the community, which his death would create, and the need to preserve what he had created by ensuring its continuity through the kind of leadership that would identify with him and his work. Indeed, history is too full of instances when the achievements of great people have been ruined by quarrelsome or unworthy successors who come to power by virtue of heredity. The history of the founding fathers of the Jewish people, however, shows that the really great made sure that their successors carried on with their own lifestyle and work because they were worthy by reason of merit, not hereditary right, to be designated their successors. Thus, for example, Abraham chose Isaac, Isaac chose Jacob, Jacob preferred Joseph, David, Solomon. All were the younger sons but in the eyes of their fathers, the more worthy ones to carry on with the work. Rabbi Judah did the same. Even though his eldest son, Gamliel, was entitled to be the prince, Rabbi Judah wanted

---

15. Because of the Hadrianic and other oppressions of the Jews after the Bar Kochba rebellion in 133–135 C.E., Rabbi Judah the Prince wrote down the Oral Law–the *Torah shebe'al peh* and divided it into six parts–*shishah Sedarim*–the first letters of which make up the Hebrew word *shas*, by which the Talmud is often called. The work of Rabbi is the *Mishnah*. It was finalized toward the end of the second century C.E. See *Mavo Hatalmud Lerabbi Shmuel Hanagid*, chap. one ". . .The *Mishnah* is that which is called the Oral Torah. . . . Judah the Prince . . . wrote it down in order to preserve it lest it be forgotten by those who study it and be lost."

16. *Ketubot* 103a.

to point out that that entitlement was not the reason why he appointed him to that position. Indeed, he was aware that his other son was the wiser one, and therefore it could be argued that he should be the real leader of the people. However, the reason Rabbi Judah appointed Gamliel to be the prince was that even though he was not as wise as his father, while Simeon was, nevertheless he was as God fearing as Rabbi Judah was. This was more important. Therefore he was the worthier of the two sons to be the head of the people.[17] Fear of God, in other words, is a greater and more meritorious qualification for leadership than the possession of sheer wisdom. Simeon was wise, but Gamliel feared God; therefore Gamliel was chosen to lead the people.

The same applied to Chaninah bar Chama. He was chosen to be the head of the academy because of his piety and knowledge. Chaninah bar Chama proved that later on, when he refused to sit in the presence of one whom he considered to be a greater scholar than he was. One of the attributes of the God fearing is that they do not serve God or the people for reasons of personal gain or recognition. They do it for the sake of heaven. Consequently, they avoid arguments, public intrigues, and personal gain. They preserve the peace. That is why those who are God fearing are preferred to those who are merely wise as public leaders.

How God fearing and wise Rabbi Judah was. What a legacy of public service he left behind. He also left a legacy of faith and trust. In his death he taught us what he believed in and how he viewed life. It is upon those principles of faith that he based his own way of conduct. Rabbi Judah's requests not to be dressed too much for burial and to have a perforated coffin teach us his views concerning life, death, and the afterlife.

The request to be buried in a simple shroud and not in many garments indicates that Rabbi Judah scorned the prevailing custom of extensive and lavish funerals, which exemplified the belief in materialism and an afterlife in which the luxuries of this world continued to play a role. By his request for a simple funeral, Rabbi Judah indicated that in the world to come, the materialism of this world plays no role and that the afterlife is only a spiritual one.[18] There is no one there who

---

17. Rashi on *Ketubot* 103b. See also the Commentary of the *Rashbah* on *Ketubot* 103b.

18. *Talmud Yerushalmi, Ketubot,* op. cit. See the discussion by the commentators Korban *Ha'eidah* and *Penei Moshe* and also *Tosefot* on *Ketubot* 111b. The *Talmud Yerushalmi* mentions that Rabbi was buried in a shroud. The custom to be buried in a shroud (*Tachrichin*) is attributed to Rabbi because he did not want the people to go into great

is impressed by our material wealth and accomplishments in this world. Only the spiritual accomplishments are of value there. Therefore a shroud is enough. There are also those who say that the reason the rabbi requested not to be buried in many garments was that such garments usually delay the decay of the body and multiply the vermin. This is obnoxious for the body and causes pain to the soul, which hovers around the grave as long as the body has not yet disintegrated.[19] Because of that, Rabbi Judah also requested that his coffin have a perforated bottom, so that the body, by coming into contact with the earth and the moisture, would disintegrate as quickly as possible and thus fulfill what is written in the Bible, namely, "From the earth thou hast come and unto the earth shalt thou return."[20] The sooner this is accomplished, the sooner the soul will find its rest and dwell in peace in heaven.

We conclude from this that Rabbi Judah believed fervently in the survival of the soul, the supremacy of the spiritual over the material life, the relationship between the soul and the body, and the accountability of the soul for its deeds here on earth; that the sooner the body disappears, the sooner the soul can be released from its responsibility here on earth; and that the material life in this world is fleeting.

Rabbi Judah left a legacy during his dying hours alone that others could not achieve in a lifetime. He approached death as if it were the departure for a journey into eternity. He left his house, his family, his public affairs, and his duties in order as he departed from this temporary world of change, tug and pull, and constant flux and went in the direction of the eternal world of stability, quietude, and consistency. He lived a life of steadfast faith. He entered the new world with a serene sense of certitude in his continued spiritual existence and place in heaven. How blissfully he must have left. How at peace he must be now.

He was a great teacher during his lifetime. He taught people how to live and how to die. May we be privileged to learn from him how to do both.

---

debt over the funeral preparations, which he regarded as being wasteful and a wanton destruction of property—*Bal tashchit*—which is prohibited by the Torah (Deuteronomy 20:19). According to *Moed Katan* 27b and *Ketubot* 8b, Rabban Gamliel is credited with starting the tradition of being buried in a shroud: "At first the burial of the dead was more difficult for the survivors than his death. It reached the point where the relatives would leave the corpse (in the street) and run away. Until Rabban Gamliel came and humbled himself by being buried in a linen shroud. The people followed his example and were, thereafter, also buried in a linen shroud."

19. *Shabbat* 152b–153a.
20. Genesis 3:19.

9

In His Presence

The quest for eternity is a human trait. Not only do we have a desire to live forever, but we also wish to know who among us will achieve it. To put it in other words, we all want to know what enables one to live forever in this world or to enter into Heaven in the world to come.

In the Talmud[1] we are told by Rabbi Abahu that King Solomon, the wisest man of all, was asked, "What kind of man will live in heaven?" He answered, "Anyone of whom it says, 'before his elders shall be glory.' "[2]

What does it mean? There are several possible interpretations. The commentators on this verse of Isaiah 24:23 state that the prophet tells us that at the end of days, when the Messiah will come, "The elders of His people will receive glory from the nations of the world."[3]

According to this interpretation, only such people who are similar to those who would be worthy enough to be glorified because of their virtues by the nations of the world at the time of the coming of the Messiah are going to Heaven. Such a definition would limit the world to come to only those few who are indeed the elders of God's people.

Rashi, however, offers us a different interpretation. He defines the

---

1. *Baba Batra* 10b.
2. Isaiah 24:23.
3. Radak (Rabbi David Kimchi) on Isaiah 24:23.

elders as those people who are being honored in this world because of
the wisdom of their age. There are old people and there are old people.
Some are old in years. Others are old in wisdom. Those who are old in
wisdom will continue to live in heaven. Their lives do not stop at the
grave. They have lived here wisely. They have acquired passage into
the next world, the world of the soul and the world of wisdom.

According to Rashi, Solomon tells us that anyone who attains the
status of being a wise old man will enter into heaven.[4]

There is yet another interpretation of this verse.

The Maharsha says that the Hebrew phrase in question reads,
Neged zekeinav kavod–in opposition to his elders is glory. That is, the
word "elders"–*zekeinav*–has to be read as being the opposite of its
counterpart, which is youth. Therefore, the verse should read thus:
"He is glorified in his old age who is also glorified in his youth."
Therefore the passage means, "He who lives such a good life during his
youth that he has nothing to be ashamed of when he grows old will
also be glorified because of it in his old age. Such a person will continue
to live in heaven."[5]

What a beautiful interpretation! What a beautiful life one must
have been blessed with in order to know that in youth one was as good
as in old age! What a strong will one must have possessed to have
overcome all the temptations of youth and life! How wise one must
have been to have avoided all the pitfalls of daily existence! Such a one,
indeed, deserves to go to heaven. One who in old age can look back on
middle age and youth and say, "I have led a straight life throughout my
years on this earth," is a blessed one.

Yes, there are such people.

Yes, they deserve heaven and they go to heaven.

What a comfort it is to know and to believe that such people exist
and that heaven is their eternal resting place.

Indeed to be in His Presence is their glory!

---

4. Rashi on *Baba Batra* 10b.
5. Maharsha on *Baba Batra* 10b.

10

"Rabbi Meir, Why Weren't You Rabbi Meir?"

There is a great story, told in the name of the *Chafetz Chayim*,[1] one of the great and pious teachers of recent years. His real name was Israel Meir Kagan. This is what he used to say.

When the time comes, and I depart this world and will be brought before the heavenly throne for judgment, I will be asked, like everyone else is, many questions. However, I am not afraid of any of them, because I will always have a good answer. For example, we are taught that all of us should strive to be like Moses our teacher. Well, should I be asked, "Why weren't you like Moses?" I will say, "Because we lived in different times, under different circumstances. Times and people were not the same. Family responsibilities were too demanding, and so on." Indeed, any question that I will be asked I will be able to answer one way or another. That includes questions about riches and social status. However, there is only one question I am afraid of. That question is, "Rabbi Meir, why weren't you Rabbi Meir?" In other words, why wasn't I myself? Why didn't I live to my own fullest capabilities? Why didn't I give the soul that was entrusted to me on this earth its full and complete realization and fulfillment? Why didn't I live

---

1. This is how I heard the story first from my revered teacher and mentor Rabbi Dr. Abraham Kravetz, zt"l, of Winnipeg, Manitoba, Canada. However, there are those who attribute the story to other sages and not the *Chafetz Chayim*..

to my full potential? This is the meaning of the question. "Rabbi Meir, why weren't you Rabbi Meir?" This is the question he was afraid of.

Indeed, this is the question every person should be afraid of, not only at the end of our life, but throughout our entire journey here on earth. If at the end of time we can depart this world and answer the question all of us must be asked or should be asking ourselves—"Am I myself?"—with the answer "Yes, indeed, I was myself; I did my best; I lived to the fullest of my abilities," then indeed we have nothing to fear.

The trouble is that so many of us spend a lifetime trying to be like somebody else. We do things others are doing. When the time comes to answer the final questions we are able to acquit ourselves very well on those questions that ask us how well we did in life or why we did not become like everyone else, but we do very poorly on the question of why we were not ourselves. The great *Chafetz Chayim* taught us the lesson that we need not fear our failure not to be the way others are, but instead should fear the question that demands of us why we were not ourselves.

If at the end of time we can look in a mirror and say, "I was myself," then we need not fear.

If at the departure of each of our dearly beloved regardless of how old or young they were, we can say they were themselves, that they truly and really always were themselves to the best one can be, we need not mourn. Their destiny in heaven is ensured.

11

The Beauty of Creation

The more meaningless an event, the more difficult it is to understand. The less we understand the purpose of things, the more we have trouble accepting them. The more purposeless and meaningless a death, the less we can understand and accept it. It would seem that, on the continuum of the various ways death occurs and brings sorrow and pain to mankind, the most meaningless and purposeless one is that of a stillborn child or one who dies in infancy. Why? What harm did it do? Why allow the expectant mother to go through the nine months of pregnancy and the travail of labor only to see the fruit of her womb dead or die? Why raise the hope of the mother and father and then at the moment of its fulfillment snatch it from their grasp?

Perhaps such death and suffering is so far out of the reach of human comprehension that in order not to admit man's inability to cope with it, it has to be denied as having any reality altogether. Thus Jewish law, strictly speaking, does not regard a newborn baby, for mourning purposes, as being a full person.[1] Therefore, the laws of mourning do not apply to it.[2] Who, though, would dare tell a mother

---

1. That is until the age of 30 days, as in the case, for example, of a *Pidyon Haben* (*Yoreh Dei'ah* 305:11)

2. *Shulhan Aruch, Yoreh Dei'ah* 344:4, 8 (New York: Otzar Halacha, 1959). See also Beth Hillel commentary on ibid., 344:4.

and father that their precious gift was not a full person? Who would dare suggest that their pain is any less than that of a parent whose child died at an older age? If so, what then was the purpose of such a birth and such a death?

All people and all things have meaning and serve a purpose!

The creation of a stillborn or the death of a newborn also has meaning and purpose. These, too, can teach a mother and father a very important lesson. They teach a mother about the beauty of pregnancy, of carrying a life within her, of being a partner in creation. Even though the infant did not endure, nonetheless creation it was. Indeed, we are told that before this universe of ours came into being, God created many other universes. Each one of them was in turn destroyed until finally ours remained.[3] Each one of the destroyed universes was, in its own right, no less a universe than ours, which remains. It was no less created by God than ours was. Yet none survived. The birth of a child, even if it does not survive, is no less a birth. It came to teach the mother and father of the beauty of their creative power, of the excitement of expectancy and anticipation, of the wonder of life. To be able to do this for others is also a noble purpose in life. An infant who dies serves that purpose.

That baby also served another purpose. It gave notice to the parents and to others that life should not and must not be taken for granted. No matter what we do, unless God contributes His share, we labor in vain. This little babe, therefore, in death, taught us the great lesson of how precious, fragile, and uncertain life is. Such a little one teaches us through death how tenderly we must treat those who survive.

A mother and a father who have been afflicted with the pain of losing an infant should look at these great lessons and the beautiful experience their baby brought them by merely having been born. That little baby taught them such a great lesson! Surely that little child's birth had a purpose. That is why the death was not in vain, just as the birth was not. The parents were not put through a hollow experience. They were taught a great lesson—the lesson of the marvelous beauty of creation!

---

3. *Midrash Rabbah*, Genesis 3:9, "The Holy One created worlds and [then] destroyed them."

12

Sandcastles

The great and saintly *Chafetz Chayim*[1] compared this world to a sandcastle and the people who live in the world to children. He said that children who play in sand and make sandcastles have no greater joy. To them their castle is the world. It is their power, their accomplishment, and their possession. There is no greater thing than the castle they built. Indeed, there is nothing else. When their castle is destroyed, their entire world is destroyed with it. How true!

How many of us remember our own childhood and the castles we built in sand? How proud, how good, and how happy we felt at our great accomplishment, and how sad and totally devastated we became when a wave washed our castle out to sea, or a bully stepped on it and turned it back to sand, or someone accidentally squashed it underfoot. Our world came to an end with it. We cried, we were sad, we thought nothing would ever take its place. Unfortunately, life is the same to many of us.

When our dear ones die, we believe that the world for them and for us has come to an end, and there is nothing more left. We become devastated, just as we are crushed when our childhood sandcastle was destroyed.

---

1. David Zaretzky, "The Sand Castle," *Yated Ne'eman* (6 *Kislev* 5751/23 November 1991), p. 6.

Fortunately, however, we should, and some do, know better. This world may indeed be a sandcastle, and adults may sometimes be like children, but life is not, and we have the ability to see and grasp more than children do. Adults should understand that there is a difference between life and the world. In this world, all of us build and live in our own sandcastles. Now they are here and now they are gone, but life goes on beyond. Unlike the sandcastles, life cannot be destroyed by wind or storm, by brutality or ignorance. Life continues beyond.

In this world, our life may come to an end when our body dies. Like the sandcastle, the body cannot endure. Our soul, our spirit, however, continues to live, even after our body is gone. Indeed, our body is no more than a sandcastle, but our soul is life eternal.

Many of us look upon life the way children do. When their castle is destroyed, their whole life is destroyed. When their body is dead, they think *all* of life has come to an end as well, and there is nothing left. Some of us, however, know better. We know that a sandcastle is just a sandcastle and no more. Its destruction does not bring the world to an end. We know that our body is just a body. Its death does not bring our life to an end. We continue to exist outside of it and beyond it. The same way that the castle we built as children was nothing but a pile of sand, albeit beautifully shaped, so our body is nothing but a handful of clay, even though beautifully fashioned. Its destruction brings only the shape of the clay to an end. We continue to live beyond. We go to the world of the souls, the world of heaven, the world of eternity.

That was the great message of the *Chafetz Chayim*. That is what all who are grieving can take comfort in. Our body is like a sandcastle, but our soul is our life. It lives forever!

13

The Peacemakers

In the 1970s, it was in vogue to write and talk about human experiences in the life beyond this world. There were many personal and clinical accounts of experiences and visions by people who were on the verge of death or were presumed to have been dead and who recovered, recounting their visions and feelings in the life beyond. Many listeners found comfort in these accounts and gained encouragement for their belief in an afterlife.

Joseph, son of Rabbi Joshua, we are told in the Talmud,[1] went through such an experience. He was ill and fainted. His father and the other people around him thought he had died. After he recovered he told them about the visions he had while unconscious. He said that he heard the angels saying, "Happy is he who comes here in full possession of his learning."[2]

Time and again we read how the sages emphasize the importance of learning, not only in this world but also in the world to come. Why is this so, and what does it mean?

Perhaps we might find an answer in what learning does. According to the rabbis, learning leads to peace.[3] There is no greater goal

---

1. *Baba Batra* 10b.
2. Ibid.
3. *Berachot* 64a

45

in life than to maintain and create peace in the world.[4] This is true of all peace; peace between and within nations and communities, in families, between wives and husbands, and between parents and children. The ultimate goal of all virtues is to bring peace. When God wanted to bless the Israelites, He blessed them with peace. In order to maintain peace it is permitted to tell a white lie.[5] Peace in a household is a blessing. One must go out of one's way to maintain peace among neighbors, religious groups, and communities.[6] The ultimate goal of scholars is to promote peace in the world. The greatest compliment paid to Aaron the High Priest is to say that he "loved peace and pursued peace"[7] and furthermore, that everybody should be his disciple and do the same.[8] Indeed, God Himself promotes peace on earth as He does in heaven.

Scholars who die and come into the next world in full possession of their knowledge, that is, in full control of what they have learned, which must of course mean that they have also practiced peace on earth, are therefore to be highly rewarded. Consequently, they shall enjoy happiness in heaven.

Not only scholars, however, can pursue peace. The pursuit of peace is open to everybody alike. The rich and the poor, the weak and the strong, the wise and the simple can all pursue peace. Any man or woman who is blessed with the desire, inclination, and courage to pursue peace will indeed be counted a happy person in heaven.

Happy are those who pursue peace. They will be long remembered on earth and live forever in heaven!

---

4. *Midrash Rabbah, Vayikra* 9:9, "Peace is so great that before God created the world he made peace between the heavenly and the earthly beings."

Avot 1:18, "The world stands on three pillars: truth, justice, and peace, as Zechariah said: 'In your gates you shall judge with truth and justice of peace' " (Zechariah 8:16).

Midrash Tanchuma on *Vayikra Parshah* 7: Great is peace because God seals the priestly blessing only with "peace." Indeed the very name of God is Peace (*Shabbat* 10b) and it is equal to all other blessings (*Torat Kohanim* on *Bechukotai* 26:6, and see also *Mishnah, Shevi'it* 4:3).

5. Rashi on Leviticus 18:13. See also *Midrash Rabbah, Vayikra* 48:18 and *Kalah Rabbati* 10:1. There are other sources as well.

6. *Gittin* 59a–62a (Vilna: The Widow and Brothers Romm, 1920).

7. *Avot* 1:12.

8. Ibid.

14

Enough for a Grave

There is a story about a man who worked very hard all his life, trying to eke out a living. His livelihood consisted of working the fields for a nobleman.

One day, in a mood of magnanimity, his master said to him, "I would like to reward you for your faithful service and devotion, and set you free in a tract of land of your own. Therefore, I will give you as much land as you can cover in one day. You can have only the land you will cover by going out and coming back during that day, from sunrise to sunset."

The man was delighted. The next morning, he set out at the break of dawn and walked as fast as he could. He walked and ran and walked again. He felt as if he were being carried on wings by the mere thought that at nightfall he would be his own free man and a landowner. He walked and ran and walked again. He did not stop to eat. He did not stop to drink. As the day progressed and the sun rose, it became warmer and then hotter. He took off his jacket and his shirt, to keep cooler, but he still wouldn't rest. He kept walking and running. He did not want to stop because he knew that with each step he would gain a little more land, so he kept on going until he looked up and realized that it was well past midday and it was time to turn back, but, no, he would walk just a little more. It then became a little more and a little more, until the sun began to set. In fright, he turned back and began to run. He was beginning to panic lest he would not return before sunset and so his entire day's hard work would be in vain. In fear and under stress he began to run. To make it easier, he took off his undershirt. He ran. He took off his overpants. He ran. He took off his shoes and socks. He ran. The perspiration was pouring down from all over his body. His breathing was getting harder and harder. His feet were getting heavier and heavier. The pain in his legs was becoming unbearable. His pace was slowing down and down. The sun was setting faster and faster. It was almost beyond the horizon. He still had some distance to go. His strength was going and finally he collapsed. He fell. He couldn't move. His heart was giving out. His body was aching all over. Suddenly it all stopped. He was dead.

At nightfall, when his faithful servant did not show up, the master went out looking for him along the path on which his servant had set out in the morning. He did not have far to go. Not far beyond the village, he found the body. Turning to his companions, he said, "What a pity. He was such a nice servant. He was so eager to become rich. Now, give him enough ground for his grave. He doesn't need any more."

So they buried him where he had fallen and gave him all the land he would ever need, enough for his grave.[1]

There is a powerful message in this story. So many people spend their life working and running, trying to acquire worldly possessions and riches. In the process, they have no time for anything else. In fact, in the course of the pursuit of their goal, they become so involved with themselves and their single-minded goal in life that they strip themselves of all human qualities. Much the way the hero of our story stripped himself of all his garments, they strip themselves of all other concerns. In the end, they, too, end up with only enough possessions for a grave. Such people ignore family and friends, community and country, and often even themselves. They are too busy running against the sun. No one, though, can outrun the sun. In the end, it always overtakes us.

When one has lived in such a way as to have shared one's life, time, love, possessions, wisdom, and understanding with one's family

---

1. I heard this story many years ago. It is based on a tale called "How Much Land Does a Man Need?" by Leo Tolstoy. See Leo Tolstoy, *Stories and Legends*, trans. Dorothy Canfield Fisher (New York: Pantheon, n.d.) p. 45.

and friends, community and country, then one has acquired all one can on the racecourse of life. Such a one has won the race against the sun. At the end of the days of life, such a one will not fall and die, naked of all virtues, with only a grave to one's name. Such a one will depart from this world fully dressed in all the good one has performed, the love given, and the reputation left behind.

There are many such people. Your dear one may have been one of them. How comforting it must be to know that this in fact is so.

15

The Body Language of the Dying

Body language may be defined as the science of the study of human bodily reactions in relation to human thought and feeling. Today, it is commonly known that the way people move their body is a sign of how they think and what they feel. What they do is a reflection of their innermost emotions and thoughts. This is now accepted. However, it is really not new. In antiquity, human behavior and human thought were regarded as one, not only in terms of symbolic language but also in emotional reactions. What is more surprising is that the concept of body language was applied also to the study and interpretation of the meaning of messages transmitted by the dying. In the Talmud, we are told that the position of one's body and the disposition of one's attitude, such as a smile or a tear at the time of dying, are indications of what kind of destiny awaits the person after death. Thus, the body language of the dying sends a message to survivors and is also an indication of what the dying one believes is waiting in the world to come. It is a testament about one's life on earth. The body language of one on the deathbed is also an indication of what kind of reception one may expect in heaven, as one's soul is about to depart from this world. These ideas are embedded in a series of statements that Ben Azai makes about the meaning of the body language of a man on the verge of death. They are brief. They are cryptic. Says he:[1]

---

1. Ben Azai, *Avot Derabbi Natan* 15:1–2 and also passages 1–28.

1. "When a man dies while his mind is at ease because of his wisdom which he has acquired, it is a good sign for him." Such a man has both knowledge and manners. His learning did not make him arrogant. He lived a life of faith and humility until his end. It is a sign he will go to heaven.

2. "When he dies with his mind not at ease, it is a bad sign for him." It shows his knowledge went to his head. His manners did not improve. He was forbearing and of little faith. It is a sign that he will have trouble in the world to come just as he is troubled here.

3. "When a man dies at a time when he is at peace with his desires, it is a good sign for him." It shows that his inclinations and passions are in harmony with his mind and understanding, and therefore he must have a clear conscience, because he led a good life. He need not worry about what is awaiting him in the world to come.

4. "When he dies while his mind is not at ease with his desires, it is a bad sign for him." It indicates that he is concerned about his past behavior and is unsure whether he lived by what is right or by what his inclinations told him. He has reason to be worried!

5. "When a man dies at a time when he has the respect of the sages, it is a good sign for him." It shows that he is behaving properly and has earned the high regard of the wise men. He was able to do so to his dying day and need not fear the world to come.

6. "When he dies at a time while he does not have the respect of the sages, it is a bad sign for him." This shows that even though he may have been held, at one time, in the high opinion of the sages because of his conduct, he has lost that opinion now because he must have somewhere gone astray. Indeed, life is full of such experiences. For example, Yochanan the High Priest lived a life of impeccable piety and righteousness and yet, at the age of eighty, became a heretic.[2] One can never tell what tomorrow may bring until one's dying day!

7. "When one dies with his face directed upward, it is a good sign for him."[3] This shows that he has a clear conscience and is prepared to meet his Maker without fear. Such a man will surely go to heaven. He can look straight forward.

---

2. See the Commentary on ibid., by *Binyan Yehoshua*.
3. See also *Ketubot* 103b.

8. "When one dies with his face turned downward, it is a bad sign for him."[4] This obviously indicates that he is ashamed and is hiding his face. He is afraid because of his past misdeeds. It is an admission of one's guilt.

9. "When one dies with his eyes looking straight at the people around him (at his deathbed), it is a good sign for him."[5] This shows that he is at peace with them, and being thus at peace with his fellow men, he is also at peace with his Maker.

10. "If his eyes do not look at the people around him when he dies, it is a bad sign for him."[6] It shows that there is no peace between him and them. He must feel guilty about his deeds toward them and cannot face them. Therefore, he cannot face God either.

Indeed, it is Jewish doctrine that God cannot forgive us for misdeeds against our fellows. That, only people can do.[7] Therefore, unless we come before God with a clean slate about our actions on earth, we will not be accepted. Thus, Ben Azai emphasizes the importance of setting our life in order on Earth, so that we might be able to enter into heaven.

11. "When a man dies with a happy countenance (laughing), it is a good sign for him."[8] That means that he already has a glimpse of the Divine Presence and is delighted to enter heaven. Indeed, some interpreters maintain that this is the real meaning of the biblical verse "no mortal can see God and remain alive."[9] That is, after being in the presence of God no one wants to return to earthly life. One who, on one's deathbed, glimpses the Divine Presence is so happy that he no longer wants to return to life. Obviously, such a person must have led a good life to be worthy of being greeted by the Divine Presence so quickly.

Phenomena like this, such as people who are happy to enter into the next world and are reluctant to turn back, have

4. Ibid, in *Avot Derabbi Natan,* "*panav zekufin.*"

5. Ibid, *Kalpi Kotel,* "Facing the Wall."

6. *Yoma* 85b (Vilna: The Widow and Brothers Romm, 1920). Ramban. *Mishneh Torah, Hilchot Teshuvah* 2:9, and the Commentary of the *lechem mishneh* on the same. See also *Baba Kama* 92a.

7. *Ketubot* 103b, *panav tzehuvin ve'adumin.*

8. Exodus 33:20.

9. Ibid. See Rashi.

been known to occur. There are many such accounts in books on the subject. I was once personally told such a story by a noted surgeon who was very sick. He told me he was sure he had been dead and was very happy in that state. He was reluctant to return to life. When people leave this world with a cheerful countenance, they may be sure they are entering heaven.

12. "If one dies with a frowning (crying) face, it is a bad sign for him." This shows that he is unhappy to leave this world because what he sees awaiting him is not good. He is afraid of the future and he knows he has reason to be afraid.

13. "When a person dies with a clear mind, it is a good sign for him." This shows again that not only were all his affairs in order during his lifetime, but even at his last moments in life, he is able to put everything in order.

14. "If he dies in a state of confusion, it is a bad sign for him." This shows that his entire life was not in order and he is now overcome by what awaits him.

15. "When a man dies while speaking, it is a good sign for him." It shows that he is in command of the situation and not overcome by fear of the future.

16. "If he dies while being silent, it is a bad sign for him." Obviously, he keeps quiet because he has nothing to say. He cannot speak about his past, present, or future. His lifestyle was such that there is nothing to say about it. Now he must keep silent.

17. "When one dies while speaking about the Torah, it is a good sign for him." Since the Torah is eternal and the study thereof is one of the highest virtues, surely one who was engaged in such labor must deserve to receive the full reward for doing so, and the reward is a place in heaven.

18. "If he dies while being engaged in business affairs, it is a bad sign for him." Business represents the material world and transient existence. Such a man, to his last moments, showed that he preferred the material pleasure to the eternal, spiritual values. Therefore, he may not go to heaven immediately.

19. "When one dies while engaged in the performance of a good act, it is a good sign for him." What greater indication can there be of one's religious nature?

20. "If he dies while performing a worthless act, it is a bad sign for him." What greater testimony can there be that he lived a worthless life than being caught performing a worthless deed?

21. "When one dies in the midst of a happy atmosphere, it is a good sign for him." It shows he led a happy life and was not deterred, even by bad events. Whatever God gave him he accepted happily.

22. "If he dies in the midst of sadness, it is a bad sign for him." It also shows that he was always unhappy and did not accept the vicissitudes of life gracefully. He therefore did not accept God's decisions willingly and was of little faith. Such a person cannot be expected to be rewarded in heaven.

23. "When one dies while laughing, it is a good sign for him." It shows he always accepted God's decrees willingly.

24. "If he dies while crying, it is a bad sign for him." This shows that he has a guilty conscience. He either has committed transgressions or has not been able to accept his lot in this life and thus rebelled against God. Now at the moment of truth, he is aware of it and cries because it is too late to make up for the past. He is afraid of what awaits him.

25. "When a man dies on the Eve of Sabbath,[10] it is a good sign for him." It shows that he will enter into peace in the world to come, because Sabbath represents rest and peace.

26. "If he dies at the end of the Sabbath day, it is a bad sign for him."[11] It indicates that work, travail, and uncertainty lie ahead for him.

27. "When a man dies at the end of the Day of Atonement, it is a good sign for him."[12] It shows that all his sins have been forgiven because that is what happens on Yom Kippur.

28. "If he dies on the Eve of the Day of Atonement, it is a bad sign for him."[13] It shows he is going to be judged and may not be forgiven.

---

10. Ibid.
11. Ibid. See Rashi.
12. Ibid.
13. Ibid.

If you want to know what kind of life your beloved led and what awaits them in the future, watch their state of mind and facial expressions at the time of death. Body language may tell you volumes you never dreamed of![14]

---

14. The question of death as perceived by the dying is raised by Robert Jay Lifton in *Death in Life–Survivors of Hiroshima* (New York: Random House, 1967).

In the footnote on page 489, he says that Wisman and Hackett in "Predilection to Death and Dying as a Psychiatric Problem" (*Psychosomatic Medicine* [1961], 23:232–56) suggest a concept of appropriate death, from the standpoint of the dying person, as having four principal requirements: conflict is reduced; compatibility with ego ideal is achieved; continuity of important relationships is preserved or restored; and consummation of a wish is brought about. Insofar as survivors can consider such criteria to be applicable to a particular death, their guilt may be minimized. But they are likely to have even more difficulty looking upon that death as "appropriate" than the dying person himself. Perhaps the advice of the Talmud might be of help to the survivors in overcoming their dilemma.

16

How Great Is Man!

Death is the ultimate blow to one's sense of justice and demand, which comes from the innermost recesses of the soul, for righteousness as well as the need to perceive a balance, in both the social and cosmological orders of the universe. Only when one has faith in an afterlife in which ultimate justice is executed, equality before the law implemented, no favor shown, and no quarter given, can one find the answer to the fundamental question, "Why? Why all these trials and tortures of our life?" Faith in an afterlife can be very comforting to the bereaved because it gives assurance that their dearly departed is now in the presence of the Almighty, before whom absolute truth reigns, all questions are answered, and all suffering is made worthwhile.

Rabbi Elazar Hakapar laid down these guidelines, for both a more philosophical life and a more sanguine approach to death. He said, "Those who are born will die; those who are dead will be resurrected. Those who are alive will be judged in order that they should know, teach, and become conscious that He is God, He is the one who fashions life, He is the Creator, He is the Discerner, He is the Judge, He is the Witness, He is the Plaintiff, and He will, in the future, pass judgment. Blessed is He, before Whom there is no inequity, no forgetfulness, no favoritism, and no acceptance of bribery, because everything is His. Know that everything is according to the reckoning. Do not allow your evil inclination to assure you that the grave will be a place of escape for you, for in spite of your will were you fashioned, and in spite of your will were you born, and in spite of your will are you alive, and in spite of your will will you die, and in spite of your will will you have to give an account before the King of Kings, the Holy One, blessed be He."[1]

What a powerful way of summing up the quintessential issues of life. What a succinct way of delineating the limitations of human existence on the one hand and extolling our greatness on the other. Imagine that that helpless creature, which came into being, lives, and dies against its own will, is at one and the same time great, beautiful, and strong enough to stand in the presence of God and, what's more, give an account of itself and its doings? How magnificent a creature we must be, to be worthy to stand before God and utter, "I know You! I am aware of You! Truly Thou hast made us but a little lower than the angels!"[2]

Man is blessed with all of these after death. Surely, then, death, the passage from momentary life to one of an eternity, must not be so bad after all.

Indeed, how can death be bad when it leads to the ultimate fulfillment of our potential? Perhaps if we think of death in the same terms as we do of the pangs and pains of birth, when the fetus passes from the womb – and its temporary life – into the world – and a life destined to be so much better and greater – we will fear it less and be comforted more.

May our awareness of the fact that in death our departed stand in the presence of God instead of man, bring us comfort and consolation forevermore!

---

1. *Avot* 4:29.
2. Psalms 8:6.

17

A Mother

"He who has a mother is blessed by God," says the famous Jewish song, popularly known as *"Ein Yiddishe Mame."* Indeed, it is so. However, only one who is an orphan can really appreciate what it means to have a mother. To have a mother means to have somebody before whom you can cry without shame, to whom you can complain about a million and one insignificant as well as important things in life. A mother is a confidante, a friend, a guide, a teacher. A mother is a nurse and a doctor. A mother means that you are not alone, that you have roots, that you have a family to come to. A mother inspires and disciplines you. A mother holds out promises for your future. From a mother you don't mind receiving a complaint or a compliment. A mother is the world to you because she gave it to you when she bore you. She diapered you and nourished you. She gave you love, compassion, and understanding. She built up not only your body but also your mind and your ego. She was indeed God's partner in creating you. No wonder we are told to honor our father and our mother.

The rabbis were trying to outdo each other in showing respect for, love of, and honor of their mothers. Rabbi Tarfon would bend down whenever his mother wished to climb into her bed or when she wished to descend from it, so that she could step onto him to make it easier for herself. Yet, when he told, with pride, about it to his friends, they said to him, "You have not reached half as much of the honor owed to her.

58

Had she thrown a purse containing money destined for you, in front of you into the sea, without your yelling at her and thus putting her to shame, then you would have shown her due honor![1] Rabbi Tarfon felt embarrassed. When Rav Yosef used to hear the footsteps of his mother, he would say, "I will rise for the approaching Divine Presence!"[2]

Rabbi Tarfon thought that by serving his mother personally, he did her honor. His colleagues, however, said as long as it did not cost him anything, it is only half the honor due her. He should do more in order to fulfil the commandment to "honor your father and your mother."[3] However, Rav Yosef's statement could not be disputed. Indeed, it is the ultimate honor to compare one's mother with the Divine Presence, because in fact she is to be compared with it. Didn't the sages teach us that "there are three partners in the creation of man, God, one's father, and one's mother"? When man honors his father and his mother, the Holy One said, "I consider it as though I dwelt amongst them and they bestow honor upon Me!"[4]

To honor one's mother is to honor God because she, too, like God, has had a share not only in creating us, but also in shaping our life and standing by us when we needed her most. Rav Yosef had it right when he rose up for his mother as though he rose up for the Divine Presence. Just as there are no limits to our honoring God because of all He does for us, there is no limit to our honoring our mother for all she does for us. Can we ever honor her enough?

Rabbi Yochanan said, "Happy is the man who has not seen his parents."[5] Rabbi Yochanan's father died after his mother conceived him, and his mother died when she bore him, we are informed in the Talmud. Therefore, not having any parents, Rabbi Yochanan ironically says happy is the man who has not seen his parents and therefore does not have to worry about extending the proper honor due to them in fulfillment of the commandment to honor them. This is one way of looking at the meaning of what he says. Another interpretation may be that consequently, one need not worry whether or not one has properly fulfilled God's commandment to honor parents, for this

---

1. *Kiddushin* 31b (Vilna: The Widow and Brothers Romm, 1920).
2. Ibid.
3. Exodus 20:12.
4. *Kiddushin* 30b. See also the Commentary on the above by the Maharsha.
5. *Kiddushin* 31b.

commandment is so important. Indeed, it entails also the honor of God Himself, not only of one's parents. Therefore no one can ever be sure that one has discharged the duty to honor father and mother, and therefore also God, one hundred percent.[6] Better never to be put to the test than to fail it. That is what Rabbi Yochanan meant by his statement.

When our mother dies, this test is over, but the test of our conscience is just beginning.

When mother was alive, did we treat her well? Did we take her for granted? Did we honor her? Did we appreciate her? Did we take notice of all she did for us—her self-denial, her pride in us, the early mornings and late nights she woke up and waited for us? Each of us knows what we meant to our mother and what our mother meant to us. Now she is gone. Are we paying due respect to her memory, or will her days come to an end as she enters the grave?

The psalmist asks of God, "Will the dust acknowledge you, will it declare your truth?"[7] God can meaningfully be acknowledged only among the living. Our mother, too, can be properly remembered among ourselves only. She has to be honored in this world. Children can never do enough to honor the memory of a mother. On the other hand, they can take comfort that now, after death, she is no longer here, representing God in partnership but instead representing herself to ourselves on the one hand, and us before God, on the other.

She will not change her role in that life. She will continue to be our mother in spirit, there in heaven, as well as she ever was in body, here below on earth.

------

6. Ibid., Rashi.
7. Psalms 30:10.

18

To Be Judged as One

There was a time when many people believed in the separate existence of the body and the soul (there still may be such people today). Certainly, some believed that the spiritual and material are two separate entities, which operate independently of each other, and that the coexistence of the body and soul within one person is merely accidental. They also believed that if this were to be taken to its logical conclusion, one could escape all Divine Retribution and thus, responsibility for one's actions here on earth, which, of course, would lead at worst to a totally anarchistic or at best to a totally hedonistic social order. Under such a philosophy of life, all morality would be meaningless and all actions and modes of behavior acceptable. Death would mean merely the separation of soul from body and an opportunity for one to escape all responsibility for life heretofore. The dead would gain freedom from the restraints of life in this world and the survivors would have, therefore, no cause to mourn.

A debate along these lines took place some nineteen hundred years ago, between Judah the Prince and Antoninus (some say he was Marcus Aurelius). Antoninus approached Rabbi Judah and said to him, "The body and the soul may escape judgment by placing the blame for their misdeeds in this world on each other. How so? The body will say, 'the soul has sinned, for since the soul left me I am lying like a dumbstone in the grave (and do no wrong).' The soul will say, 'the

61

body sinned for since the day the body left me, I am flying like a bird in the air (and do no wrong).' " Rabbi Judah replied to him, "Let me answer you with a parable. To what can this be compared? It can be compared to a mortal king who had a beautiful orchard, which contained delicate figs. He appointed two watchmen to guard the orchard. One was lame and one was blind. One day the lame said to the blind, 'I see delicate figs in the orchard. Come and take me upon your shoulders and we will pick the figs and eat them.' So the lame man rode on the shoulders of the blind one, and they picked the figs off the trees and ate them. After some time, the owner of the orchard came and asked them, 'Where are my delicate figs?' 'How do I know?' answered the lame man, 'Do I have feet to walk with?' The blind one said, 'How do I know? Do I have eyes to see with?'

"What did the owner do? He placed the lame on the shoulders of the blind and judged them together as one. Similarly," continued Rabbi Judah, "the Holy One, blessed be He, will bring the soul and put it into the body and pass judgment on both of them at one and the same time, for it is written, 'He shall call to the heaven from above [this refers to the soul] and to the earth that He may judge His people [this refers to the body].' Some interpret the verse to mean that 'the earth' means 'body,' and the word '*amoh*' – 'his people' – is read instead as '*imo*' – 'with him.' Therefore, the verse means, 'He will call the soul from upon the heavens to judge it (together) *with* the body from the earth.' "[1]

Thus we see that there is no escape from Divine Judgment. Though the body and soul may argue, like the blind and the lame did, that they are in and of themselves incapable of committing any evil (or any good for that matter), God has shown that together they are a potent force. The grave is no escape from responsibility here on earth; neither does the ever-unfolding process of life, started at birth, terminate when the soul and body part from each other. Life continues and with it continues the responsibility that comes with it. Human behavior makes a difference here – below – as there – above.

When we lose dear ones, we should know that their life does not stop at death. They continue in the world to come. Death is merely a change of dwelling places. Life is stronger than the grave. It is more than the body or the soul in and by each one of them alone. Life is the sum total of the body and the soul together. What the two have

---

1. *Sanhedrin* 91a–b.

wrought here on earth is what they are to be judged for there in heaven. This world is a passage into the world to come. As the sages said, "This world is like a vestibule and the world to come is like a palace. Prepare yourself in the vestibule so that you will be able to enter the palace."[2]

Remember your dear ones are now in the palace of eternal life, reaping the rewards for all the good they did during their lifetime! May they continue to do good in heaven!

---

2. *Avot* 4:21.

19

He Fulfilled What Is Written

How comforting it must be to survivors to know that their dear departed was a person who lived up to some standards that society holds in high regard. On occasion one does come across a man or woman of excellent character and high esteem who lived by a code of conduct to be envied. How lucky are the survivors when everybody is praising the virtues of their father or mother.

I once knew such a man. He came from humble beginnings. By hard work and high integrity he rose to economic and social status. Though parted by war from his family, he never forgot them. When the time came, he brought them over from the war-ravaged country, settled them in jobs and houses, and showed them love and affection as only a father could. He equally loved his elderly parents. Unlike the common fashion of placing old parents in an old age home, he kept his in his own home and made extra provisions for their care and comfort in their old age. All of this was not easy. It was an extra burden on him, but he did it with love and did not begrudge his brothers, who in time rose to high social office in his community because of his own standing. We can all point to such people, especially among the immigrant societies and generations whom we know. Such persons, alas, also die. When this particular one passed on, I delivered his eulogy and found the following story especially appropriate. His relatives and friends found it very comforting.

64

Throughout all the years that the Children of Israel wandered in the wilderness they carried two arks side by side. One was of Joseph's coffin, and the other one of the Divine Glory (the Law). When passersby saw these arks, they would ask, "What is the nature of these arks?" The answer came, "One of them contains the coffin of Joseph and the other one the Divine Presence [the Law]." The people would then query further, "Is it proper for the dead to be walking next to the Divine Glory–the Law?" Again they were answered, "Yes, because this one [Joseph] fulfilled what is written in the other one–the Law."[1]

The commentators explain that Joseph fulfilled not only the Ten Commandments but also the additional laws of the Five Books of Moses, which were all contained in the ark.[2] When Jacob died, Joseph continued to show brotherly love toward his entire family.[3] He comforted his brothers.[4] He did not avenge their former hatred of him. He kept them alive. He sustained them and provided for their care.[5]

How wonderful it is to depart this world and leave behind a reputation that can be compared with that of Joseph the Righteous. The person I spoke of was also such a man. How lucky are his survivors that they can be comforted by the knowledge of the wonderful legacy, reputation, and name that their dear father, brother, relative, and friend left behind. How fortunate are such relatives, who will always be able to read upon his tombstone the wonderful message: "This one fulfilled what is written in that one."

May his memory be a blessing even as his life was!

---

1. *Sotah* 13a–b (Vilna: The Widow and Brothers Romm, 1920).
2. Rashi on *Sotah* 13a–b, quoting the *Midrash Mechilta* on *Shemot, Vayechi Beshalach.* See also the Maharsha on *Sotah* 13a–b..
3. Genesis 50:19–22.
4. Ibid.
5. Ibid. Note the Commentary of the Maharsha. The behavior of Joseph toward his brothers was in keeping with the laws of the Ten Commandments.

20

Happiness Awaits Him

All people fall into a great middle group called average. Give or take some social status, money, cultural refinement, success in life, and a little health and you have a picture of all men and women. On occasion, though, you come across a really exceptional human being: one who has good manners, gives charity, is kind and compassionate, never has a bad word to say about anybody, and does not engage in gossip, yet leads a life of deprivation and plain suffering. I have known such people, who are usually described as righteous human beings, yet who had a life of personal suffering. Do you know such people? I had to bury such a man.

He was a quiet, unassuming man. He went about his business quietly and honestly. He always set a certain amount of profit, just enough to pay his expenses and enough to make a gain on the merchandise he sold. He always observed all the ritual requirements, closing his business on the Sabbath and Festivals. He gave charitably both to various organizations and to private individuals. He was active in his community. He gave his children a good education and a good home. He was a kind and attentive husband. He honored his parents and relatives. Yet he had trouble: He was sick. He had ulcers. He had other complications. He died of cancer at a relatively young age. His was not a kindly death, if ever death can be kind. How to comfort his family? They ask, "Why? Why did he die so young? Why did he have to suffer in his last days? We know everybody dies, but why did he have to have so much pain the last days of his life? Couldn't he go in peace at least?"

These are hard questions to answer. They raise problems. And they are unfortunately not new questions. We have had to live with them ever since we became aware of God and capable of articulating our thoughts about the pain of life. The rabbis asked this question in their customary subtle way by wrapping it in a parable. Said Rabbi Elazar ben Rabbi Tzadok,[1] "To what are the righteous compared in this world? To a tree," he answered, "which is standing wholly in a clean place and one of its branches is overhanging an unclean place. When this branch is cut off, it remains standing in the wholly clean place. Thus, the Holy One, blessed be He, brings suffering upon the righteous in this world, in order that they should be able to inherit the world to come, as it is said, 'and though your beginning is small, in the end, you will grow very big.' "[2]

The interpreters[3] of this passage say that the question means this: "To what are the righteous who suffer to be compared?" and the answer is, "To a tree which stands in a wholly clean place." That means we are compared to a tree, as it says, "for a man is a tree of the field"[4] because just as a tree produces fruit on its branches, so, too, do we produce fruit through our actions. Furthermore, just as a tree may be wholly strong and good but might have a rotten or sickly branch, so, too, might a wholly righteous person have some transgressions. These transgressions are compared to the branch that overhangs the unclean place. Just as by cutting off this sick branch of the tree the tree will remain standing in a wholly clean place, so, too, by punishing the righteous person for the few transgressions committed, which may have been even unwitting, the person will become wholly righteous and thus be able to enter the world to come without any encumbrances. Like the tree pruned of the bad branches becomes wholly healthy and produces only good fruit, the righteous, purified by affliction in this world of some of their transgressions, become totally righteous and enter the world to come, where a whole life of bliss is

---

1. *Kiddushin* 40b.
2. Job 8:7.
3. Rashi and Maharsha on *Kiddushin* 40b.
4. Deuteronomy 20:19.

awaiting them. The passage from the Bible should not read, "though your beginning is small" – *tzar* – but instead of small, read "troubled" – in the end you will grow very big."[5]

Pain and pleasure, death and birth, are part of the mystery of life. Life as we know it is imperfect, or else we would have no death. Goodness, happiness, and health are merely stages and stations on our journey to life eternal. The same is also true of their opposites – evil, sadness, and sickness. They are all transient moments in our life. No one can go through life being at all times in all places and under all circumstances wholly good, happy, and healthy, or, conversely, totally evil, sad, or sick. Human beings are by definition changing beings. Only angels, we are told, are static and never change. When they do, they fall. When people change, they make progress. Our great strength is that we can change. We can go up or down. That is also our great weakness. When we go up, we become better. When we go down, we fail in the mission to improve ourselves and the world around us. When we go up, we improve both ourselves and everybody around us. However, none of us has ever reached perfection, otherwise we would stop going upward. To be human means to be not perfect.

The righteous are only that, righteous. They are not perfect. However, God loves them for their righteousness. He wants to reward them for it. He, therefore, removes all our imperfections by punishing us for our transgressions and thus prepares us for an eternal life of happiness.

When the righteous suffer, be sure the suffering is to their advantage. Their reward awaits them in heaven. There they will know only goodness forevermore!

Take these words to heart, and be comforted!

---

5. Maharsha, op. cit.

21

Welcome in Peace

The death of the righteous people leaves a mark in this world and creates an impression in the world to come. Indeed, it is as though they are expected in the world to come, and great preparations are made there for their welcome. Heaven's gain is earth's loss.

Said Rabbi H. Chiyya bar Gamda in the name of Rabbi Yosi ben Shaul,[1] "When the righteous departs from this world, the ministering angels say to the Holy One, blessed be He, 'Master of the universe, such and such a righteous man is coming,' whereupon He says to them, 'Let the righteous ones come and go out to welcome him and let them say to him, "He enters into peace, they rest in their beds." ' "[2]

What does this greeting teach us?

We see that not only the ministering angels but God Himself takes the trouble to welcome the righteous into heaven. It is God Who tells the righteous who are already there what to say. His message is clear. The righteous are welcomed into heaven, the place of peace. They enter into peace itself. Only after they are welcomed and made to rest in peace can those who go out to greet them return to their own places in peace. Until then, they must minister to the welcoming of the righteous into heaven. When their task is finished, they may return to their own rest.

---

1. *Ketubot* 104a.
2. Isaiah 57:2. The text reads *"shalom"*—peace—not *"beshalom"*—in peace.

It is also possible to read this greeting as meaning that after their arrival in peace, the righteous will rest in peace forever in their beds.[3]

One commentator (Malbim) says that this biblical passage with which the righteous who are already in heaven greet the new arrival is a reply to those who question the meaning and purpose of life when they see that the righteous die just as the ordinary people do. Therefore, in order to be properly understood, the meaning of the greeting must be taken in the context in which the prophet Isaiah – from where the verse is taken – states it in the first place.[4]

Isaiah opens his remarks by saying, "The righteous man perishes and no one takes it to heart, and pious men are taken away and no one thinks that it was because of the evil (which is yet to come to the world) that the righteous was taken away."[5]

This means that when people see the righteous die they do not understand that it is because God wanted to spare them the suffering which is to come to the world[6] and not because they were guilty of some sort of evil doing, as people often think. Indeed, when we see upright, pious, and righteous people die, it is because God is saving them from the pain that they would suffer at seeing the trouble of the world. Therefore, God tells the prophet Isaiah to say, "He enters in peace," that is, the righteous dies in order to come in peace into the World of Peace. The pious die in order to find rest in the World of Eternal Rest, because all of them enter in uprightness to the place where they are destined to receive their reward.[7]

It is this that God tells the ministering angels to instruct these righteous people who are already in heaven to proclaim when they are sent to greet the righteous upon their departure from this world and welcome them into the next one.

Those people who are pursuing justice, performing loving-kindness, serving mankind and God alike, even though they may be ignored during their lifetime and forgotten at their death, are nevertheless recognized and remembered by God for all they did in this world. They are rewarded in the world to come. There are people who are

---

3. Rashi on *vayavo beshalom* in *Ketubot* 104a.

4. Rabbi Meir Leibush ben Yechiel Michael Malbim on Isaiah 57:2 in his *Bi'ur Ha'inyah* in his *Sefer Torat Elohim*.

5. Isaiah 57:1.

6. Rashi on Isaiah 57:1.

7. Rashi, ibid., and Malbim, op. cit.

ignored in this world because they dedicate their life to serving God and therefore are not noticed by their fellows. Their death leaves no more an impact on society than their life did. There are other people who also work only at helping society and who do receive public notice and are popular. But when they die, their death only confuses people, who ask why should such a one die. In the end, however, both of these groups of people, no matter how they were treated on earth, are welcomed by God and His ministering angels into peace and into heaven.

The moral of this story is this. There is reward after all for righteous living, pious conduct, and loving-kindness. Death need not be viewed cynically as the end of all. It need not lead us to conclude that there is no justice and there is no Judge. On the contrary, if we lack understanding, God does not. If we cannot appreciate the value of these good people, the ministering angels can. They will always be there to proclaim the praise and the welcome of the righteous ones who lived on earth when they are welcomed in peace in heaven!

22

The Treasured Tears

Mourning for the dead is a great virtue. It tells you something about the nature of those who mourn. It teaches you what they think of human beings and how they value human life. It shows you what they believe about the human soul. It reflects their thinking about the place the deceased occupied in this world and the role he or she played in life. It shows whether or not the departed will be missed by those who survived. Mourning, crying, and weeping for the dead also indicate what we think of ourselves. They are a mirror reflection of our own self-image.

The sages teach that "Any person who weeps and mourns at the death of another human being who was a good person is forgiven for all his sins because of the honor which he has done to him."[1]

How great must be the virtue of weeping and mourning for a good person when it overcomes all the sins that one might have committed in a lifetime! How great must be the worth and life of a single human being that to recognize it is such a great deed that it merits forgiveness for all our sins! Indeed, how great and wonderful must be the miracle of life itself that when death strikes it down, it is as though the greatest act of evil has been committed and by recognizing this fact through our weeping and mourning, we also recognize that

---

1. *Moed Katan* 25a (Vilna: The Widow and Brothers Romm, 1920).

nothing in life is equal to it! Therefore, all our sins are forgiven, for in the presence of death, nothing else matters. When we mourn, we recognize this fact.

Indeed the extent to which we mourn is an indication of the extent to which we appreciate the value of life. In the Jewish tradition there is no object which is venerated more and held in greater esteem and awe than the Torah. When it is destroyed, it is a cause for bereavement and mourning.[2] One must fast and tear one's outer garments as a sign of mourning. The Torah is a symbolic expression of the presence and word of God. There is nothing holier than it. Yet, the rabbis teach us that "Any person who is present at the expiration of a soul must rend his garments. To what is this compared? To a scroll of the Torah which was burned."[3] In other words, the death of a human being is as great a loss as the Torah scroll because they are both equal. A human being is as important, is as holy, and is to be revered as much as the scroll of the Torah, which represents the Word of God!

Rabbi Shlomo Yitzchaki explains the analogy in this way. People are compared to a scroll of the Torah because "the Torah is called 'a lamp' for it is written, 'for the commandment is a lamp and the Torah is a light,' and it is written, 'the lamp of the Lord is the soul of man.' "[4] How wonderful! We carry within us the spirit of God. When one dies, it is as though that spirit, that light of God, which is in everyone, and, through the person, in the entire world, were extinguished. What greater cause is there to mourn than that one – the death of godliness with the death of each one? Surely, then, we can now understand why one's sins are forgiven because one honors one's fellows by weeping and mourning for them. For in doing so, we weep and mourn for the death and loss of godliness in our world.

The same rabbi, Shlomo Yitzchaki, states elsewhere concerning the same analogy between the scroll of the Torah and a human being that "the soul taken from any Israelite is compared to a scroll of the

---

2. *Shulchan Aruch, Yoreh Dei'ah* 340:37. He who sees a scroll of the Torah burned . . . tears his (outer) garment twice. The *Shach* (Rabbi Shabetai ben Meir Hakohen) comments: "The same law applies in the case when it is torn, cut up, erased on purpose (Gilyon Maharsha: to spite, *lehachis* . . . everything depends on one's seeing the profanation of the Name." See also *Sanhedrin* 60a and *Moed Katan* 26a.

3. *Moed Katan* 26a.

4. Rashi on *Moed Katan* 26a.

Torah because there is no one among the Israelites who has no Torah and no good deeds."[5] There is no person, in other words, who does not have some good in him. Every person is a walking divine spark. When our soul leaves us, the Divine spark is also extinguished.

No wonder the Talmud says,[6] "Whosoever sheds tears at the death of a good man, the Holy One, blessed be He, counts them and stores them away in His treasure house, for it is written, 'You have counted my wanderings, put my tears in your flask; are they not already in your ledger?' "[7] God treasures the tears of the brokenhearted, especially those who mourn for the dead, because He knows how dearly they hold life and how much they value the miracle of God's presence in every human being. One commentator[8] states that when we weep at a death, it is a sign of our own fear of heaven. That–the fear of heaven–is the only possession which God has given us that we can call our own. The sages teach us that "Everything is in the hands of heaven, except the fear of heaven."[9] The fear of heaven depends on our own freedom of choice. We may or we may not have fear of heaven. It all depends on us. Therefore, the only true personal gift that we can offer up to God is our own fear of God. It is the most genuine, pure, humble, and personal gift that we can bring to God. That is why God accepts it and treasures it more than anything else. Indeed, there is nothing else. Everything else belongs to God in the first place. Only fear of God is a true gift of people to God. There is no greater fear of God than the fear expressed at the death of another good human being. It brings out in us our realization of our own mortality and anticipation of the day of our own reckoning. Who can think of that day without a shiver running down the spine or fear in the heart? When we weep and mourn at the death of another person, our grief is genuine, if only because it is an expression of our own fear of heaven. Such tears are genuine. They deserve to be stored in God's Treasure House.

There is also an opinion, expressed by Rabbi Pinto,[10] that these

5. Rashi on *Shabbat* 105b.
6. *Shabbat* 105b.
7. Psalms 56:9.
8. Maharsha, op. cit., on *Shabbat* 105b.
9. *Berachot* 33b.
10. Pinto, Yoshiahu ben Reb Yosef (*Meor Einayim*), *Harif* on Perek He'oreg, *Shabbat* 105b. In the *Ein Ya'akov Hotza'at* Safra (New York: Shulsinger Bros., 1944): p. 96, ". . .He places them [the tears] in His House of Treasures in order to use them for the resurrection of the dead for the Holy One, blessed be He, resurrects the dead with dew

tears will be used by God in the future to water the grounds for the resurrection of the dead. What a beautiful thought! The tears shed at the passing of the dead will be used to revive the dead. True poetic justice! Those who mourn at the loss of life surely deserve to be the first to be part of the creation of life.

The opposite is also true. Anyone who stands by the death of another and neither mourns nor feels the pain of the loss of the divine in our midst, neither does that one understand the grandeur and miracle of human life. Such a person is callous and brutish and lacks the human qualities that differentiate us from beasts. Some rabbis spoke in the harshest of terms about such people. Rabbi Judah said, "Whosoever was lazy and did not properly eulogize a scholar deserves to be buried alive,"[11] for it is written, "and they buried him [Yehoshua] in the border of his inheritance in Timnat-Serah, which is in the hill country of Ephraim, on the north of the mountain of ga'ash"[12] (ga'ash also means "volcano"). Rabbi Judah, therefore, deduces from it that the volcano erupted and threatened to kill the Israelites (because they did not properly eulogize Yehoshua). Thus we see that the penalty for not eulogizing a scholar (which Yehoshua was) is death. Obviously the reason for this is that a scholar represents divine wisdom and human accomplishment. A scholar's death cannot be ignored. Those who do not see this are unworthy of being human themselves, for what else can we do or think if we do not realize the grave loss of another person, especially one who is, so to speak, filled with the spirit of Divine Wisdom?

Rabbi Chiyya bar Abba says,[13] "Whosoever is lazy and does not properly eulogize a scholar does not continue to live long because of the

---

[batel] because it says, 'Your dead shall live, my dead bodies shall arise, awake and sing; you dwell in the dust, for your dew is as the dew of light' (Isaiah 26:19). That is to say, the tears which come from the light which are the eyes, those tears are the dew of the eyes which are lights. That is what is meant by 'talecha lehachayot hameitim' [Your dew is for the resurrection of the dead]. Therefore he puts them in His Treasure House in order to use them for the resurrection of the dead for it says, 'You have counted my wanderings.' It [the word 'nod'–wanderings] comes from the expression 'lanud lo,' which means to weep. 'Put my tears in your flask; are they not already in your ledger?' means to count, that is to say, God counts the tears and puts them in His Treasure House, for it is written, 'Put my tears in your flask,' that is, store them away in a hidden and safe place."

11. *Shabbat* 105b.
12. Joshua 24:30.
13. *Shabbat* 105b.

principle of 'measure for measure,' as it is said, 'In full measure when you send her away you contend with her.'" According to Rabbi Kimchi,[14] this means that God judges the Israelites in direct proportion to their sins. In other words, the punishment fits the crime. Others (Rashi) say that this verse means that according to the same measure by which the Egyptians afflicted the Israelites, they themselves were judged at the time when God took the Israelites out of Egypt.[15] Thus we see Rabbi Chiyya bar Abba's justification of his statement that "Whosoever is lazy and does not properly eulogize a scholar does not live long," for they, too, will be punished by the same measure as they measured the dead one. They did not mourn the death of the scholar, obviously, because they did not think the scholar's life was important, nor did they consider the scholar a loss; consequently, their life will not be regarded as important either, and their death will likewise not be considered a loss. They did not miss their fellow and God will not miss them. How tragic! If only we realized how interdependent is our life with all others, how much we are linked with the dead, how much our consideration and appreciation of the existence of others mean for us also, how differently would we act, how different we and our life would be.

Yes, indeed, how bad it is to lose a dear one, but how good it is both for the departed and for us that we have been endowed with the capacity and ability to mourn the loss. In mourning we pay tribute to our loved one and do good for ourselves. When we mourn and shed a tear, it shall be stored away in God's Treasure House. It shall yet revive the dead in the future and prolong our life in the present!

---

14. Isaiah 27:8.

15. David bar Yosef Kimchi, ben Kimchi Hasefaradi (Radak), Commentary on Isaiah 27:8.

23

The Lost Pearl

Who are the losers when death occurs? When we believe in the survival of the soul and eternal spiritual life, surely death is not the end of life. It is only the end of our journey on this earth. Who then must be the losers? Surely it must be the survivors. Those who loved and no longer have their loved one with them, those who benefited from the loved one's care, concern, hard work, and good advice and who no longer can have it are the losers. The survivors are the sufferers. The dead merely changed dwelling places.

Rabbi Elazar said in the name of Rabbi Chaninah, "When a righteous one is lost, that one is lost to a generation. This can be can be compared to one who lost a pearl. No matter where it is, it is still called a pearl. It is lost only to its owner."[1] Indeed, only the owner can feel great loss. The same is also true of the righteous. Wherever the righteous are they remain righteous beings. Only the generation that has lost the righteous knows the pain of their absence.

Rabbi Elazar, according to a great rabbi's explanation[2] of his story, tells us in this short and beautiful parable that the souls of the righteous remain forever. Only their body dies here on earth. They continue to live in heaven forever. Their departure is a great loss, though, to their

---

1. *Megillah* 15a (Vilna: The Widow and Brothers Romm, 1920).
2. Maharsha, ibid.

generation, for by their death the survivors have lost the source of wisdom, righteousness, and goodness that they bestowed on them. Therefore, they should mourn the death for their own sake, and not for the departed's, whose destiny is secure. But the destiny of the survivors, because of the death, is now weakened. They must worry about their own future.

The same is also true of a family situation. When the head of a family dies, the family must worry about themselves and their future. Who will take care of them? Who will guide them? Who will show them right from wrong? The one who died need not worry. Like the righteous, like the pearl, wherever the departed is, the departed will reap reward. The soul is now in heaven, and life is now eternal. The survivors, like a city bereft of its righteous and the person who lost the pearl, must now worry for themselves. The family alone can feel the depth of the pain of the loss, the suffering of separation, and the fear of sudden responsibility for all they have to do that has fallen upon their shoulders.

One thing, though, in which they can take comfort, is that the one who was taken from them, like the righteous, is now in heaven. Another is that that one will continue to care for them from up above, even as he or she cared for them here below. That, too, is comforting!

24

The Dead Who Are Alive

In an age of relative values it is difficult to draw comfort from the mere observance of reality. Only when values are clearly marked can one draw some sort of comfort from the mere observance of the vicissitudes of life. When evil and good are clearly defined, it is possible to see whether the righteous suffer and the wicked are punished or vice versa. When life has purpose and direction, it is possible to say who is going on the right path and who is not.

The rabbis, for example, teach that "the righteous people are regarded as being alive, even when they are dead, but the wicked people are regarded as being dead even when they are alive."[1] Why is this so? Of course, because the rabbis base this statement on a passage of Scripture. In fact they have several such sources. One of them is, "and Benaiah the son . . . of a living man."[2] Whereupon they ask, "Are all other people then the sons of dead men?" "Rather," they respond, "the son of a living man means that even in his death he was called living."[3] As to the death of the wicked, one of the biblical verses upon which they base their interpretation is this one: "and you, O wicked one, that are slain, the prince of Israel."[4] That is, even though

---

1. *Berachot* 18a–b.
2. II Samuel 23:20.
3. *Berachot* 18a–b.
4. Ezekiel 21:30.

79

the prince is still alive he is already called slain, as though it had already taken place, and he is dead, while in fact he is still alive.

Why, however, should the sages call the wicked who are alive, dead, and the righteous who are dead, alive? One explanation is simple and obvious. The wicked people lead an empty life. Their whole existence consists of the pursuit of negative goals. They are destructive; they are harmful; they take all they can from life; they return nothing; they contribute nothing to the improvement of life or people or society. Their existence has neither purpose nor value and is of no substance. Therefore, even though they are alive, they might as well be dead. However, the righteous people are the opposite. They give; they strive to improve the world; they support and help their fellows; their existence contributes to the welfare of society and the improvement of the lot of mankind. Their life has value, purpose, and substance. What they do during their lifetime will live even after they are gone. Therefore, even when they are dead, they are alive. Indeed, the righteous, the more they are aware that they are going to die, the more they try to live a more righteous life and consequently the more they are preserved in this world after their death. The wicked, however, never pay attention to the fact that they are ever going to die, and as a result they never attempt to change or to improve their personality or their deeds, so that even when they are alive their life is of no value and is meaningless. They are, therefore, dead even while still alive.

When people are concerned with death and life and with grief and bereavement, it is worthwhile to think in terms of absolute qualities of good and evil, right and wrong—in short, what life is all about—and then to ask ourselves how we fit into it also.

If we have done all we can, if we have lived a life and continue to live a life of doing good, then we can be sure that we, too, have some right to continue to live in this world, even after we die. The same is also true of the ones we mourn. The more good they have done, the more we can be sure they are still alive in this world! May the things we know of them bring us comfort!

25

The Captain of the Ship

When a head of state or a leading personality dies, it is not unusual that the whole nation or often even the whole world is thrown into a state of grief and sorrow. I remember as a child during World War II – when the news reached us in our small Belorussian town that President Franklin D. Roosevelt died – how the principal of the school called an assembly and dismissed the entire school as a sign of mourning. Frankly, as a child, I don't remember having known much, if anything, about Roosevelt, but I still remember the sad, even teary, face of the principal as he announced this grave news of the death of the great friend and leader of the world. I still carry a picture of that event in my mind to this day. Why is it then, that the world mourns the great?

The sages tell us that Rabbi Chanan ben Rabba said, in the name of Rav,[1] that "On the day when Abraham our father departed this world, all the great men of the nations of the world stood in line and said, 'Woe to the world that has lost its leader, woe to the ship that has lost its captain.'" The commentaries[2] explain that the leaders of the world have made two distinct comments because there is a difference between mourning the loss of the leader of the world and the captain of a ship. They both represent two distinct ideas.

---

1. *Baba Batra* 91a–b.
2. Maharsha on *Baba Batra* 91a–b.

The leader of the world is a reference to Abraham's knowledge of and faith in God, the One and only God. Abraham was famous for his preaching and the proclamation of his faith in the One and only God. He was the herald of monotheism. In this sense, he is referred to as the leader of the world, that is, the one who taught mankind the knowledge of, and faith in, God. However, as captain of the ship, he exemplifies other traits, that is, the traits of morality and integrity. Just as the captain of a ship is guiding it through the waters of the sea by carefully steering it in order to avoid all sorts of difficult obstacles in the sea, so, too, Abraham guided mankind on the right path of life by teaching the right moral values and showing the righteous path upon which to go. The ship represents life. The sea represents the currents of life. The captain represents the one who guides humanity on its ship through the sea of life. This was what Abraham did. He was the moral leader of humanity, just as the captain of a ship is the guide of the ship through the waters of the sea.

When the leaders of the world paid tribute to Abraham, our father, when he departed this world, they praised him for his intellectual and moral leadership. When he died, the world lost a teacher and leader par excellence. When he died, the world lost a moral guide and shepherd without equal. More than that, it lost the one who cared for its well-being as no one else had, the way no one else cares more for a ship than its captain does. Therefore, the world mourned its loss and his departure. In his departure, all the world was diminished too.

When a great leader of a nation dies, that nation loses not only a great person but also a guide. It suddenly becomes like a ship without a captain. Therefore, it is important on such occasions for nations to stay their national course and pursue the path that their leader has set them on, or else they might become lost the way a ship may be lost at sea. Great leaders are seldom replaced. Greater leaders seldom fade from memory. They continue to live because the nation follows on their path. When this takes place, death does not separate the two. It merely integrates the teachings of the leader into the hearts and conscience of the people.

Happy are the leaders whose destiny this is.

Happier still are the people who were blessed with such leaders.

26

The Topsy-Turvy World

Why do the wicked prosper and the righteous suffer? This question is as old as mankind. It takes on, however, extra weight and poignancy on the death of a decent human being who leaves behind a family bereft of friends and sustenance, for whom he was the sole provider and source of cohesion and purpose in life. How do we comfort the spouse of such a man, who turns to us with pleading eyes and a crying voice and asks, "Why him? He was such a good, gentle, harmless man. How will we live without him? Why did he have to go now? He hasn't even lived a full life." The truth is that it is hard to answer such questions. The most we can do is turn to others who may have dealt with them before and see what they have to say about it, in the hope that we might learn from them how to cope with the tragedy facing us.

We are told in the Talmud that Yosef, son of Rabbi Joshua, fainted and appeared to be dead. When he came to, his father asked him, "What did you see [in the next world]?" His son answered him, "I saw a topsy-turvy world. Those who are in this world on top are, in the next world, on the bottom. Those who are in this world on the bottom are, in the next world, on the top." His father said to him, "You have seen a cleared-up world."[1]

---

1. *Baba Batra* 10b.

Rabbi Yitzchaki,[2] the great commentator, says that the vision of Yosef refers to the position of people who in this world are held in high esteem because of their wealth. In the next world they will not be on the top but on the bottom rung of the ladder of social status. Conversely, the people who are held, in this world, in low esteem because they are poor, will be on the top rung of the social ladder in the world to come. According to Yitzchaki, status based on material possessions is of no value in the scheme of eternal life. Only spiritual qualities are of value. That includes also the quality of humility, which comes with one's being poor. Therefore, the poor will indeed be at the top in the world to come. From the fact that Rabbi Joshua said to his son, "You have seen a cleared-up world," we can deduce that his son was puzzled by his vision. His father, therefore, put his mind to rest by replying that he had seen the correct order of life.

Another sage, Rabeinu Gershom,[3] says that the expression "those who are on the bottom" refers to "the scholars who are impoverished and those of good deeds who receive no consideration" in this world. In other words, the really important things in life are the pursuit of wisdom and the performance of good deeds. These are what ultimately count. Riches have no enduring value. In this world, they may give one prominence. In the world to come, however, they are of no consequence. Only the scholars and doers of good deeds will be at the top.

There is yet a third point of view.[4] This one claims that all those of good character who in this world may suffer will, in the world to come, when the final day of judgment takes place, be blessed and placed at the top of all people.

We see from these points of view the following.

Life in this world is full of appearances. It is topsy-turvy. Only in the world to come are things sifted out and ranged in their proper order. A life of material gain and social status based on riches means nothing. Only the good life, the life of doing good for others, the life of the pursuit of wisdom – even at the risk of being scorned and scoffed at by one's fellows in this world – receives its ultimate recognition and reward in the world to come. Is this not what all of us want, after all? If given a choice, all of us would choose eternal joy, in spite of the fact

---

2. Rashi on *Baba Batra* 10b.

3. Rabeinu Gershom on *Baba Batra* 10b.

4. Maharsha on *Baba Batra* 10b.

that it may be preceded by temporary poverty, over temporary pleasure, because the latter is followed by eternal degradation.

Families who are left bereft of dear ones and who ask such questions as, "Why did this one have to die who never had a chance to enjoy life" or "Why did this one always have such a hard time?" might find some comfort in the knowledge that there are and have been others who suffered the same way but found some comfort and consolation in the belief that all is straightened out in the world to come, that not all that is good here is also good there, and that not all that is bad here is also bad there. On the contrary, the opposite is the case. We live in a topsy-turvy world. "Those who are on top here are on the bottom there. Those who are on the bottom here are on top there."

Take heart. Your dear departed may have been on the bottom here but is now on top and will stay that way forever.

May the knowledge of this bring you solace, peace of mind, and comfort of the heart!

27

When Is It Good to Die?

The hardest death to face is that of one's child, young or old. The death of any other young person is also hard. When a parent dies and leaves behind young children, people ask, "Why? What will happen to them?" When a parent dies at an older age whose children are grown up, one may say, "Well, at least they are already old enough to take care of themselves." However, when a man or a woman dies at a ripe old age, almost everybody says, "Well, they lived a full life." Or, if the death was sudden, "Well, at least he didn't suffer." Or, after an illness, "Well, at least she does not have to suffer anymore."

Is there any time when it is good to die?

The sages ask the question, "What is the difference between the death of an old man and the death of a young lad?"

Rabbi Judah said, "When a candle burns out of itself, it is good for it and good for the wick" [because it does not create any splash of the wax or soot of the flame] "but when it does not burn out of itself, it is bad for it and bad for the wick"[1] [because it creates a splash or drip of the wax and the wick begins to smoke, creating soot]. Similarly, when one dies at a ripe old age, both the body and the soul have exhausted themselves. One does not feel the pain of going nor do the survivors sense the loss as much. However, when a young person dies, neither

---

1. *Bereishit Rabbah* 62:5.

the victim nor the survivors are ready. Like the candle and the wick, the death has an impact. The dying one has disrupted his or her own life and the life of all those around him. That is why when a person dies of old age, it is a good way to die.

Rabbi Abahu compares death to the picking of figs. "When the fig tree is plucked, when the figs are ripe, that is in season," he says, "it is good for it and good for the figs; but when they are not picked in season, it is bad for the tree and bad for the figs."[2] By analogy, an old person who dies has already fulfilled his or her destiny on earth. It is therefore no loss either to the person or to the person's generation of people when the person departs from the world. Like the ripe fig, which drops off the tree without any damage to the tree, one's departure, too, is no loss to the world, but when a young person dies, it is bad for the person and bad for the world, because one has not fulfilled one's destiny in life, and the world will miss that young one's contribution to it. It is thus bad for both.

Rabbi Judah and Rabbi Abahu use different illustrations, but they believe in the same underlying principle: we come into this world to fulfil a role, for ourselves and for the world. When one dies young, one fulfills neither one's mission to fully realize personal potential as a human being nor one's task of contributing to the betterment of the whole world. One's death is therefore damaging to both oneself and society, but when one dies at a ripe old age, one has had plenty of time to fulfill one's potential in life and to accomplish one's mission for oneself as well as for the sake of the world. When such a one dies it is good for that one and good for the world. That soul can now return to its spiritual source whence it came, and the world is left a better place because that one was here.

Take comfort that your dearly departed lived to a ripe old age. Their souls are now in heaven where they belong. They accomplished their mission on earth successfully.

---

2. Ibid.

28

Why Do the Righteous Die?

Why do perfectly good people, young and old, die? Why don't the good live out their years in peace? Why do the righteous die? These questions and many more do not cease, only because none of the attempted answers are foolproof. I would like to share with you a tale that has stood the test of time, however, in the hope that its moral will help us assuage the pain these questions raise and so many bereaved suffer.

The great Rabbi Chiyya[1] and his disciples (some say it was Rabbi Akiva and his disciples, and others say it was Rabbi Yosi, son of Chalaftah and his pupils – surely this story must teach a great truth if it is attributed to so many great masters) were accustomed to get up early and go and study under a particular fig tree. While doing so, they noticed that the owner of the tree would also get up early to pick the figs. They thereupon said to one another, "Maybe he suspects us of taking his figs and therefore he gets up early to pick them," so they got up and went to another place.

The owner of the fig tree then came to them and said, "Gentlemen, there was one great merit which you bestowed upon me when you were sitting and studying under my fig tree, and now you have taken it away from me. Why?"

---

1. *Berachot* 2:8.

"Because we thought that you suspected us of stealing your figs," they replied. He appeased them and they returned to study under his fig tree. The next day, the man did not pick the figs as he always had. The sun rose and shone upon the fig tree and the figs were spoiled. When the scholars saw what happened, they said, "The owner of the fig tree must know when it is the right time to pick the figs and therefore he does it in the morning. Similarly, God knows when the time for the righteous has come to depart from this world, and He therefore removes them from it."

Thus, we all depart from this world when our time comes, which is once we have fulfilled the tasks for which we came into this world. This does not depend on the number of years we live but on how well we discharge our duties for which we were placed into this world.

Another sage[2] said that this principle is based on the interpretation of the verse in "Song of Songs": "My beloved has gone down to his garden, to the beds of spices, to browse in the gardens and to pick lilies."[3] Says Rabbi Yosi bar Chaninah, "This verse is not written correctly. It should be written this way: 'My beloved has gone down to his garden to browse, to the beds of spices to pick lilies' instead of being redundant and saying again, 'to browse in the garden' after having already said once 'gone down to the garden.' Therefore, Scripture must be telling us something extra. This is to teach us as follows, 'My beloved' means God, 'to His garden' means the world, 'the beds of spices' means His people, 'to browse in the gardens' means the houses of worship and study, and 'to pick lilies' means to remove the righteous ones from among them." Thus we see that God gathers in every person when one's time comes, just as the owner of the fig tree picked the figs when they became ripe.

In other words, when one's mission on earth is fulfilled, God calls one back to His heavenly abode. When the righteous die, it is a sign that their mission has been fulfilled, regardless of whether or not they have reached an old age. The length of years is not important for the righteous. What counts is to fulfill one's goal in life and accomplish the task God has sent one down to do. When we mourn our departed, we should think of the good they did and brought to us and those around them. This was their mission. They did the best they could. Let the knowledge of this comfort us!

---

2. *Berachot* 2:8 has a different interpretation in the name of Reish Lakish.

29

The Loneliest Death

I have seen and comforted the bereaved under all circumstances, but of all deaths, I find the death of a person who dies alone leaving no kith and kin behind the most pathetic, sad, and pitiful. How do you eulogize a person who leaves no survivors, no relatives, and no friends, to whom the only people who say the last good-bye are the one or two staff members of a nursing home and the two or three people who handle the burial? Verily such a person is a true stranger among strangers. And no one apparently knows who or what the person was.

Who can tell whether such a one was a war hero or a civilian, whether loving or loved? Did the person have a spouse, a child? Brothers or sisters? All we are told is a name, a religion, and how long the person was in this or that nursing home.

I was once notified there was to be a funeral. When I asked who the deceased was, I was told that no one knew. When I asked where he came from, I was told it was from the public housing projects. When I asked if he had relatives, the answer was no. Finally, I asked if he had a name, "Oh, yes!" was the answer. The name sounded familiar, but the person who told me was not sure. Upon investigation, I realized I knew the name and I remembered from where.

About three months before, I had been walking with a colleague when someone shouted from across the street, "Hello, Rabbi." I turned

90

and looked across the road. There before me was walking a short, scrawny little man pulling a shopping cart. He was shabbily dressed and wearing a black military cap with a brim and a Tank Corps insignia upon it. While my friend said hello to him, I looked into the cart and saw a few kosher food items, a jar of fish, a package of matzoh, and the like. I said to him, "What is your name?" He gave it to me. He also told me more.

He had moved not too long before into our town, though he was not clear how long it had been. He spoke Yiddish and recited Yiddish verse, some of which he said were his own compositions. He spoke in rhyme. He had come from Warsaw. He had served in the Polish Army of General Anders during World War II. He had been in Persia, Africa, Italy, and, finally, Germany. He then came to England, where he was living on a government pension. He had no relatives; they had all been killed in the war. He alone had fought his way through. Now he was living alone, bereft of friends or relatives – a stranger in a strange land, a foreigner in an alien community removed from both Gentile and Jew. Alone. I said to him, "Please come over; my office is just around the corner." He did not commit himself. We parted.

I felt uneasy when we parted. Is this life? Is this the reward for all the military campaigns? The sweat and sand of the African desert? The battlefields of Europe? The sheer struggle for survival and simple existence? The hell this man must have gone through during those dark days of World War II?

Now I have to bury him. What do you say at a farewell for a man like that? How do you talk to strangers about a stranger? Shall I tell them what I know about that man, that person who was a man? Who can fathom what scars were in his heart and what torment his soul endured? Who knows as he knew what it meant to be alone, lonely, and lonesome, with such a past and such a present? Now he and it are no more, or are they still lingering on in that bleak and dreary public housing or on the lively yet lonely streets on which he walked and where my memory of him lies?

How shall we say good-bye to him and the countless other similarly lonely souls who have to be laid to their eternal rest?

"Do not weep for the dead nor bemoan him who goes away," says Jeremiah,[1] whereupon Rabbi Judah said, "What does it mean?"

1. Jeremiah 22:10.

for him who goes away? "It means for him who goes away without children."[2]

Yes, indeed, and for him as well who goes away without anyone at all. That's all we can do – weep and shed a tear. How sad. How tragic. How totally meaningless life becomes and death is when there is no one to mourn. Maybe life itself is the mourner, and the sky turns gray as the heavens shed a tear. They are the real mourners, and they need our comfort. Let them then be comforted in the knowledge that we who survive will bury our dead and carry on. Life will not stop!

---

2. *Moed Katan* 27b.

30

Who Stands on the Holy Place?

When loved ones are taken away from us, we often worry what will happen to them. The tragedy of bereavement is that we have to cope not only with our own loss, our own frustration at our helplessness, and our own loneliness but also with our worries about the ultimate destiny of the one whom we mourn. What happens at the time of death? What happens after death? Does the soul exist, and if so, what happens to it? Does it come before God?

The psalmist also asks the same questions in different words: "Who shall ascend the mountain of the Lord and who shall stand in His holy place?"[1] Indeed, who?

There are actually two questions here. One is, Who shall come up on the mountain of the Lord? It implies that not everyone who goes up and reaches the top of the mountain of the Lord will remain there, even though that may be one's only goal. Yet there is an even higher goal, which is implied in the second question, Who shall stand in His holy place? That is, who shall remain in the company of the Lord in eternal bliss after having reached the top of the mountain?[2]

The answer is provided in the next lines, "He who has clean

---

1. Psalms 24:3.
2. I heard this interpretation from my revered teacher and mentor Rabbi Dr. Abraham Kravetz of blessed memory, of Winnipeg, Manitoba, Canada.

hands and a pure heart."[3] All else is simple. It does not take much to climb and remain standing on the holy mountain – only clean hands, meaning, an honest life. The hands symbolize action, involvement, and reaching out to others. If in our life on this earth we have done the right things, dealt sincerely with others, have not abused others, and have done an honest day's work for an honest day's pay, so to speak, in all our involvements with our family, our friends, our job, and our community, then we shall not only climb but also stand on God's holy mountain. We are not called upon to be wise or famous or extraordinary but only to have "clean hands and a pure heart." How easy it is to achieve. It costs no money; it requires no great education – just a simple, clean life of knowing right from wrong and acting accordingly.

If your loved ones had "clean hands and a pure heart," then you should be assured they not only ascended "the mountain of the Lord" but also stand in "His holy place." They are up there, unique in their own rights, which they earned here on earth, looking down upon us here below and thinking, "How easy it was to get here; if they only knew!" Indeed, for them it was easy, for they were of "clean hands and a pure heart."

Knowing this might make it easier for us to cope with the loss. Our loved ones are now in their rightful heavenly abode. Now we must take care of ourselves. When we do that, they, too, will help us from on high!

---

3. Psalms 24:4.

31

On the Loss of a Wife

How does one comfort a man who has lost his wife, his partner in life, the choice of his heart, with whom he toiled and hoped and dreamed, with whom he built a home and a family, and through whom he himself became fulfilled and a man of whom the Bible says, "therefore shall each man forsake his father and his mother and cling to his wife, and they shall become one flesh"?[1]

The sage Rabbi Alexandri says, "The world turns dark for any man who has lost his wife in his lifetime."[2] In other words, life itself loses all qualities of pleasure, joy, happiness, and hope. Everything which is symbolized by brightness and sunshine disappears. Without his wife, a man loses his sense of optimism and happy disposition. The world is dark. No matter which way he turns, no matter what he thinks or says, life is dark for him. How do you comfort such a man?

You comfort him by telling him to close his eyes and stop looking at the world outside. You tell him, look into your memories. Remember that before the world around you turned dark it was full of sunshine, laughter, and hope. She brought it to you, she shared it with you, she wanted you to have it. Now that she has gone, your memories of her are still with you. You still have the same responsibility

---

1. Genesis 2:24.
2. *Sanhedrin* 22b.

toward yourself as when she was with you in body. If you did things for her sake when she was alive, do it now for the sake of her memory so that she will continue to live on in this world through the legacy that she has left behind. In short, the more you live, the more she will live with you.

If your world is dark all around you, don't fight the darkness; light a candle in its midst and the darkness will disappear. Do not withdraw from the world because it is dark. Do not say, "How can I walk when I cannot see my steps?" Light a candle. Do something good for yourself and for others. You will push the darkness away. The more you do so, the more your dear wife will live on. Every candle that you light will restore the light of your life that was taken away from you. The more good deeds you perform, the more she will stand beside you as in the past, encouraging you and praying for your success.

Yes, indeed, when your dear wife was taken from you, your world turned dark. But you have the power to push the darkness away. Try it and your helpmate of a lifetime will be by your side, as always, to help you along.

32

On the Loss of a Child

As I join you in your most difficult moment of sorrow and grief, I want to reach out to you and comfort you, even though words are inadequate to express the feelings we share with you and the hurt and pain you suffer at the loss of your dear child.

Perhaps we can all find a little comfort in the following story and thus learn from other parents how they confronted the challenge of death and sorrow.

We are told in II Samuel 2:12 that King David had a little boy who was very sick and was about to die. When he first realized the seriousness of his child's condition, David tore his clothes, fasted, cried, prayed, and slept on the floor. He totally lost control of himself. Needless to say, he neglected all his royal duties. His staff understood the troubles of a concerned and troubled father and did not bother him with the affairs of state. Unfortunately, King David's fasting, praying, and pleading with God were of no avail. His beloved child died.

When the news of this tragedy reached David, he immediately groomed himself and returned to life as usual. His advisers were shocked by this strange behavior of their king. When his child was sick, he had fasted and prayed and withdrawn from life, constantly weeping and besieging God, and now that the child was dead, he was behaving as if nothing had happened. Has he gone mad, they thought!

They did not know how to face him or react to his behavior. Finally, they mustered enough courage to ask him for an explanation.

The king understood their bewilderment and responded to them quietly and simply. Said he to them, "As long as the child was alive, I fasted and prayed because I said to myself, 'Who knows, perhaps the Lord will have compassion on me and save the child.' But now he is dead; why should I fast? Can I bring him back to life? I am going to him; he will not return to me."[1]

As long as there is life, there is hope. We must all do everything in our power to save and preserve life. This is particularly true of parents. But once life has been taken, the living must go on living. You have done everything you could for your child. You have sought out all possible advice. You have exhausted your mind and your soul to help as long as there was hope. Now it's no more. Like David, you have to turn back to life.

You have to accept that you have already done all you can for your beloved child. You have gone beyond the limits of both human and parental duty. But your power is not limitless. We are all finite and must accept that. Let your conscience be clear like David's was in the knowledge that you have exhausted all of the human resources to their limits. Now it is beyond your control. Do not dwell on the past; look toward the future. You cannot bring your dear child back to you but, like David, you are going to your child. Look forward to the future. Immerse yourself in the stream of daily life! Find comfort in life itself!

---

1. II Samuel 12:22–23.

33

The New Dwelling

I have found the story of the passing of the great chasidic master Rabbi Nachman of Breslav most comforting and healing. I would like to share it with you in your hour of sorrow in the hope that you too will find consolation in its message.

The disciples of Rabbi Nachman of Breslav are known to this day as the dead *chasidim* because unlike other chasidic groups, which always have a living master by hereditary or appointed succession, the Breslav *chasidim* do not have any leader. Their master continues to be to this day their original founder and teacher, Rabbi Nachman of Breslav. Because they follow their dead master, they are known as the dead *chasidim*. But these *chasidim* may have more life in their following their dead master than some of those who do living ones. The reason why they have no successor to Rabbi Nachman is found in the story of the rabbi's death.

When Rabbi Nachman was on his deathbed,[1] his disciples came

1. On December 17, 1992, I consulted a number of Breslaver *chasidim* and scholars at the Kolel Chasiday Breslav in Jerusalem. They all confirmed the story but could not pinpoint the exact source for it in the writings of and about Rabbi Nachman. However, Rabbi Nachman Borshtein of Jerusalem, a Breslaver *chasid* and scholar, pointed out that this story is based on popular folktales about Rabbi Nachman's life and departure. The fact that the Breslaver do not have a living titular head is based on inferences and deductions of and from Rabbi Nachman's teachings and not on specific direction by

to him and asked him to designate a successor to his leadership, since he had no sons. Rabbi Nachman did not answer them, so they waited and waited, finally turning to him again and saying, "Master, you are dying and we need someone to take your place. Whom are you appointing?"

To this he replied, "No, you don't need anyone to take my place."

"But how is it possible?" they asked. "You are dying."

"No, I am not dying; I will always be with you. I am only changing my dwelling place."

This is the reason his disciples do not have a master. Rabbi

---

him. Indeed that Rabbi Nachman left no specific instructions is explicitly stated in *Yemei Moharnat*, chap. 67, p. 97. "He did not command us how we should conduct ourselves after his departure . . ." But the author continues to state that he taught them well during his lifetime how they should conduct themselves both during and after his life.

The most significant source for that story seems to be a conversation between Rabbi Nachman and one of his daughters, in which he says to her inter alia, "The death of the righteous man is comparable only to a man who goes out of one room and goes into another room." He (Rabbi Nachman, the author says) then said of himself, "It is as though I am now in this room and then I go out of this room and I enter another room, close the door behind me. If you will cry, 'Father, Father,' won't I hear you?" Similar words were heard from his holy mouth a number of times. He hinted to one and all how great will be the virtue of those who will have the merit to visit his holy and awe-inspiring grave. For he will surely listen to their words, help them, and save them from all trouble whenever possible (*Sichot Haran* [Jerusalem: Agudat Meshech Hanachal, 1985], chap. 156, p. 113).

Another significant source for the story is this. He spoke about his grave and said, "I want to remain among you—*Ich vil blaiben tzvishen eich*—and you will come to my grave side" (*Chayei Maharan* [Jerusalem: Agudat Meshech Hanachal, 1984], chap. 163, p. 173). See also p. 148, where we are told that Rabbi Nachman expressed his wish that his followers should visit his grave. See also chap. 225, pp. 192–193 for particular emphasis on the benefits awaiting those who visit his grave. However, the most pointed source for this story seems to be in chap. 64, pp. 92–93 of *Yemei Moharnat* (Jerusalem: Agudat Meshech Hanachal, 5742 [1981]):

. . . When the people (who come to pay him honor and take leave of him) saw that his end was near . . . and it appeared that he expired, I started weeping and crying out very loudly, "Rabbi, Rabbi, to whom are you leaving us?" He heard our voices, bestirred himself, and turned his head and awe-inspiring face toward us as if he were saying: "I am not leaving you, God forbid."

On p. 86 of chap. 59 in the same book, we also read:

"You may talk in my presence about my departure because I am not afraid of it at all. . . . Perhaps you are talking about yourselves, if so you have nothing to fear since I am going before you . . . you have nothing to fear."

Nachman of Breslav continues to be their living teacher and leader. He did not die. He only changed his dwelling place. He is with them in spirit and in his words of wisdom, which he taught them.

If you, too, as I do, believe in the survival of the soul after its departure from the body, you know that Rabbi Nachman was right. The dearly departed whom you mourn are not dead. They have only changed their dwelling place. In spirit they are alive. Their soul may be in heaven, but their spirit is with you. Like the disciples of Rabbi Nachman, who treat the spiritual presence of their master as real life and regard his teachings as being as fresh, as meaningful, and as vibrant as on the day he first uttered them with his mouth, you too can retain the spiritual presence of your dearly departed, by making the life you shared, the memory of the times you spent together, the work you did with one another a part of your daily life. The more you give meaning to your life with one another, the more will your loved one be with you. Remember, your dear one has only changed habitats and is alive in heaven as well as here with you!

34

The Dissolved Partnership

The death of a child, at any age, or a wife, a husband, a mother, or a father is not only a shocking and traumatic experience, shattering our emotional equilibrium, but also a jolt to our intellectual perception of reality and of life itself. Nevertheless, even if we are too traumatized when faced by death, with the passage of time, it may move us to pause for reflection about the nature of human beings and human life. In an age when our thinking and therefore also our reflexive reaction to shock are conditioned by theories of evaluation, it might be helpful to see what some of the ancient masters had to say about the meaning of life and death. Maybe there can be found in their words some help and comfort for all of us who know the meaning of death firsthand.

Years ago, the sages taught that we have three partners—God, our father, and our mother. The father supplies the white stuff from which our bones, arteries, nails, brain, and whites of the eyes are formed. The mother supplies the red stuff from which our skin, flesh, hair, and black of the eyes are formed. God provides the spirit and soul, the beauty of our features, the power of sight, hearing, speech, and the faculties of walking, intelligence, and wisdom. When the time comes for one to die, God takes His share of the partnership and leaves the father's and mother's share before them.[1]

---

1. *Nidah* 31a (Vilna: The Widow and Brothers Romm, 1920).

What a graphically poignant commentary this is on the state of human existence. Even though God and we are partners in the creation of human life, and even though we seemingly have the greater share of the partnership, how frail, helpless, and ineffectual the father and mother are in the end when God chooses to dissolve the partnership. Without God our life is no life. Without God we are only lifeless matter, truly no more than the dust from which we are created. Therefore we must realize that it is only the God-given elements within us that make the difference between our being alive or dead. Consequently, after death it is only our physical existence which ceases to be. Our God-given characteristics, which made us into a special, unique, and live man or woman must still continue to exist, albeit in a different way from the one we are used to perceiving and living with. Death is the dissolution of a partnership between God and us. The partnership was expressed in the life a person such as our beloved child, partner in life, or parent. The breakup of that partnership resulted in the removal of the élan vital – the lively qualities, which gave character, movement, and substance to our loved one. Now, after death, the body is no more, but the soul and the spirit that animated it still exist. They exist in the realm of the divine world, the world of the soul, intelligence, and eternal life.

Your loved one is now part of that everlasting world. Only the body was taken away and made part of its true nature, the physical world of perpetual change. The soul is now in the world of eternal existence. It exists. Someday we shall all be together again. Take comfort. Look to the future. Hope!

35

We Will Be There Before You

All human existence can be divided into three parts: family, work, and accomplishments. In the pursuit of happiness, if we attain satisfaction in all three of these areas, that is, if we are pleased with our family – wife, children, parents; if we are happy in our work, profession, or job; and if we are happy with our accomplishments, possessions, savings, and wealth, then indeed we are happy. Very few people attain happiness in all three areas. If one is happy in two out of the three areas of life, then indeed one is a happy person. When such people die, we say they had a good life. Yet, of what avail was it? we ask. Has all this stopped them from dying? What is life, then?

The sages approach these questions from a different point of view, which might shed new light on the problem, bring us some comfort in facing the loss and bereavement, and answer the questions we ask.

They say,[1] a man has three friends: his children and family, his wealth, and his good deeds. When he realizes that he is about to die, he turns to them for help. He turns to the children and pleads with them, "Save me!" They respond, "No one has power over the day of death"[2]

---

1. *Pirkei Derabbi Eliezer* 34.
2. Ecclesiastes 8:8.

and "No one has the means to redeem his brother."[3] The dying one then turns to his wealth and begs, "Save me!" It replies, "Riches are of no value in the day of death!"[4] When he turns to his good deeds, however, and implores, "Save me!" they reply, "Before you come for judgment, we shall be there ahead of you (to greet you!)" Thus it is written, "and your righteousness shall go before you; the glory of the Lord shall be your reward."[5]

The sages teach us several things in this story. They inform us first that of all the things we think are important in life, our good deeds are the ones that ultimately count. Second, all our achievements in this world have no power over life and death any more than we have. Third, only good deeds are of any value in life. Fourth, good deeds endure in, and survive, life in this world and are of everlasting value in the world to come.

When we stop and reflect upon our own experiences in life, do we not come to the same conclusion? If it were not for the good that people bring into the lives of each other, in particular, or into the world, in general, who would be remembered? We, as individuals, mourn the loss of our dear ones, precisely because they were dear to us, because they brought us laughter and joy, as well as help in time of need and because they performed good deeds for us in so many ways that without them our life is not the same. It is empty, meaningless, and full of sorrow. So we, who know what it is to mourn the loss of dear ones also know that it is their good deeds that really made the difference in their lives.

These are the same good deeds that not only perpetuate their memory in this world but also greet them upon their arrival in the world beyond. There they attain eternal bliss because of the good deeds they performed here on earth.

All who mourn know best the good deeds of their dearly beloved. Know, then, that the same good deeds will secure for them eternal rest in heaven as well.

Take heart in this knowledge, that your dearly departed lives on, because of good deeds, forever!

3. Psalms 49:8.
4. Proverbs 11:4.
5. Isaiah 58:8.

36

The Absolute Truth

Some philosophers define happiness as the removal of doubt and uncertainty. Therefore, the more knowledge one has, the happier one is. Thus, the pursuit of happiness is the pursuit of knowledge. It leads to the removal of all doubt. Of all human experiences, nothing is more certain, absolute, and irrefutable than death. Ergo, the presence of death confronts us with the most absolute truth. To confront death is to confront truth. All life and all meaning of life take on a different reality when death is present. When we are in the presence of a dead person, not only does his or her life come before our eyes in a different light, but so does our own self-perception and outlook on life change.

"The day of death is better than one's day of birth,"[1] said Rabbi Levy. "To what can we compare it? To two ships, loaded with merchandise, sailing the ocean. One of them was coming into port and the other one was going out to sea. The people were hailing and praising the one coming in. The people who saw this were puzzled and asked, "Why are you praising this one and not the other one?"

They answered them, "We are praising the one that is coming into port because we know that she went out to sea in peace and she is returning in peace, but the one that is now going out, we do not know what its future will be."[2] Similarly, when one is born, we do not know

---

1. Ecclesiastes 7:1.
2. *Midrash Tanchuma, (Shemot) Vayakheil* 1.

what will be the nature of that one's deeds. However, when one departs from this world, we already know of what nature that one's deeds were.

At the time of death, we know what a person is. When one is born and grows up and for as long as one continues to live, we can never be sure what one is, because people are always changing. Each of us is unpredictable. We know only what someone was yesterday, never what he or she will be tomorrow. Each of us is to that extent an enigma. Yesterday's saint may become tomorrow's sinner, or vice versa. Therefore our knowledge of anyone is incomplete at any time during a lifetime, let alone at the time of someone's birth. When a person dies, however, we know what that person was. At death, that life, such as it was, becomes complete. Therefore, "the day of death is better than our day of birth."

Just as in the case of the ships at sea, we can praise the one coming into port,because we know what it has accomplished, and not the one going out to sea, because its fate is uncertain, so, too, we can praise a dead person because we know that person now for what he or she truly was, but not the one who is newly born, because that one is still unknown to us. Thus, death gives us knowledge of our fellows.

No matter how little one did or accomplished in one's lifetime, one must have served one's purpose. There is no one who does not bring some good into the world, even if, in the worst of cases, it is hidden from before our eyes. The knowledge of that good should bring some comfort and consolation to the survivors.

37

The Conquest of Death!

Mankind's progress throughout history is due largely to the refusal to resign to life as it is. Our constant drive to change the world enabled us to turn every challenge and obstacle that we came across in the journey through time into an opportunity to create new instruments of work, open up new horizons in space, and advance our understanding of the physical world and thus use it to advantage. Because we did not accept life as it is, we advanced in science, technology, and art, developing both the body and the mind.

Medicine advanced the state of human health and is beginning to control our reproductive system. Human understanding has given new insight into life, society, and the working of the mind. In short, all of life's achievements can be laid at the feet of our refusal to accept life as it is, even to the point of challenging God Himself, as Abraham did when he stood up on behalf of Sodom and Gomorrah and demanded justice.[1] Because we refused to resign to reality as it is and always strove to overcome it, we changed the world and virtually all that is in it. We were charged to "replenish the earth and subdue it, and have dominion over the fish of the sea and over the fowl of the air, and over every living thing that creepeth upon the earth".[2] Truly, we have

---

1. Genesis 18:20–33.
2. Genesis 1:28.

fulfilled our mission well. We conquered the earth and are now conquering the heavens, too. Yet, there is one thing we cannot conquer, and that is death.

Adam ate of the forbidden fruit of the tree of knowledge and knows right from wrong and good from evil. He did not eat, however, from the fruit of the tree of life, so he must die.

Death is the only challenge we have not been able to overcome. We may, due to constant advances in medicine, hygiene, health science, and the like delay it, but we can never escape it. No matter how much we try to overcome it and how stubborn our refusal to accept it, we suffer and fight it. In the end, we must succumb to it. The knowledge we acquired from the primordial tree, whose forbidden fruit Adam ate, keeps on telling us that there must be something wrong in dying, something bad for the dead and the living, in the fact that it occurs, yet we cannot unravel that mystery and we keep on fighting it. Every time there is a death, the bereaved in their sorrow fight it, in their mourning refuse to accept it, in their silent cry of "Why?" beg for an explanation.

Perhaps knowledge and wisdom are instruments not only of conquest and constant and continued advancement but also of maturation that leads to an awareness of its own limitations. Death is that boundary beyond which not only human power but also human knowledge cannot go. We may know what death is, but we do not know how to stop it. To realize that and to accept it means that we must contravene our entire existence, which has been conditioned from time immemorial by our successful refusal to accept the reality of life as it was given to us. Mankind always managed to change reality and fashion it in its own image. To overcome this barrier created by our own experience is not to acknowledge our failure but to express our wisdom. By resigning to death we conquer death. By conquering death we remove sadness and sorrow from our midst.

"We are strangers and sojourners before you, as all our fathers were; our days on earth are as a shadow and there is no hope."[3]

"We wish it were as a shadow of a wall or the shadow of a tree!" say the rabbis, but it is only like the shadow cast by a flying bird, as it is written, "Man's days are like a shadow that goes away,"[4] which is

3. I Chronicles 29:15.
4. Psalms 144:4.

what is meant by the words "our days on earth are a shadow." The words "there is no hope" mean that none of us ever think that we will die. Indeed, all people know and even express it with their mouths that they will die.[5]

Therein lies the great comfort for the bereaved: the knowledge that they, too, will die. This awareness of one's own death is in and of itself a measure, no matter how small it may be, of comfort. If only all people realized and accepted the inevitability of death, then both dying and mourning would take on a totally different image.

Freud taught that one cannot conceive of oneself as being dead. It is that notion that may have led modern man to refuse to accept death altogether, but more recent studies such as those of Professor Robert Jay Lifton,[6] in his studies of the survivors of Nagasaki and Hiroshima, have shown that one can, indeed, conceive of oneself as being dead. Perhaps therein may be found some possibility of developing a new theory of life and consequently a new perception of death and bereavement. In the meantime, the sooner we realize that life is only "a passing shadow" and that "we shall all die," the sooner we will stop refusing the inevitable presence of death and, even though reluctantly it may be, accept its existence and bring peace of mind to the survivors.

To accept the inevitable is to conquer it.
To accept death is to subdue its inherent evil.
To subdue death's evil is to gain one's own freedom.
To gain one's freedom is to stop mourning.
To stop mourning is to start living.
To start living is to start laughing at life.
To start laughing at life is to start living in joy.
To start a life of joy is to serve God in happiness.
To do this is to attain heavenly bliss on earth!
That is the ultimate conquest of death!

---

5. *Midrash Rabbah,* Genesis 96:2.

6. Robert Jay Lifton, *Death in Life – Survivors of Hiroshima* (New York: Random House, 1967). See chap. 57, nn. 31–33.

38

Weep Sore

Many times, unfortunately, I give a eulogy and then must comfort the bereaved wife or husband whose spouse has died and with whom the survivor had shared a lifetime of experiences but with whom no children had resulted. Such a person has truly suffered a great loss. The person has not only been separated from the life's partner but also left very much alone in the fullest sense of the word. Separation is always traumatic; absolute separation is absolutely devastating. When combined with the awareness of stark loneliness and aloneness it can become unbearable.

Truly the rabbis knew whereof they spoke when they said, "The death of a man affects mostly his wife, and the death of a woman affects mostly her husband."[1] As always they found the proper verse in the Bible to support that opinion. In the first case, they cited the Book of Ruth: "Elimelech *the husband of Naomi, died.*"[2] In the second case, they cited Genesis: "When I came from Padan, *Rachel died unto me.*"[3] This they said in ordinary circumstances, when there are usually sons and daughters around. How much more so must this "effect" be on the

---

1. *Sanhedrin* 22b.
2. Ruth 1:3.
3. Genesis 48:7.

surviving wife or husband when there are no children around for companionship and friendship?

Death is much more difficult to face when one is left, literally, totally alone. How do you comfort, console, and encourage the wives and husbands who, after sharing a lifetime–often one of more than fifty years–are suddenly left alone when their husband or wife dies. Such people had only each other. Now they have nobody. Unfortunately, there are many such people.

"Weep ye not for the dead, neither bemoan him, but weep sorely for him who goes away,"[4] said Rabbi Judah, "for him who goes away means for him who goes away without children."[5] Such people truly deserve that we should shed a tear for them. They have come into this world alone and depart the world alone. Our sadness at their death and our sorrow at the loss sustained by the bereaved are therefore that much greater. I always have trouble finding the right words to say in such cases, because it hurts and pains me to see people left in total loneliness or going out of this world and entering oblivion as if they never had been. It points out only the futility of life. I look for comfort and some meaning in the word "children." Is it really possible that unless we leave physical heirs, our life has not been lived? Is it more meaningful than that of the one who lived a perfectly righteous life but had no children? Surely not! To have children means to leave something of ourselves behind, to have contributed to the world, to have reached out to people and society beyond our own self. Is there a man or a woman who has ever lived and never affected the lives of others? Can this be? Therefore, we must always search and find some good in every person who lived. As long as one has done something good, one has brought a child, in the spiritual sense, into the world. As long as one has done something good, we need not "weep sore" for that one. And the widows or widowers need not feel totally alone, for the good which their husband or wife did will always surround them.

Unfortunately, I also have the sad duty of burying those who left no "children"–either physically or spiritually speaking–and left no one who could tell of their good deeds. Of such it is said, "He who left no son does not belong among those who have a share in the world to come."[6] I would add not only in the world to come, but nothing any

4. Jeremiah 22:10.
5. *Moed Katan* 27b.
6. *Zohar*, Leviticus, pp. 430, 615.

more in this world either. How sad, how futile, how totally wasted their life must have been. In those cases, there is really very little that can be said, very little to remember, except indeed to "weep sorely," for they "went away without children" both physically and spiritually. God rest their souls!

39

The Wedding and the Funeral

There are occasions in life when joy turns into sadness, as when a wedding turns into a funeral. I remember once going to the wedding of a friend who was walking down the aisle in one room while his mother was dying in another. What do you say in a case like that? What do you do? The wedding went on.

There is an ancient story of a prominent Babylonian Jew who invited all the scholars and dignitaries to his son's wedding. While the festivities before the ceremony were taking place, he called his son, the groom, to him and asked him to go up to the attic of the house and bring down some wine from a particular barrel of great vintage, which he had saved for this special occasion. The son, respectful of his father as he was, did his father's bidding; he went up to bring down the wine. While in the attic, he was bitten by a snake and died. The father waited for his son to come down from the attic, but to no avail. Finally he went up himself to see what had happened. When he arrived at the attic, he saw his son, bitten by the snake, lying dead among the barrels of wine.

The grief-stricken father came down from the attic. He said nothing. He waited for his guests to finish eating and feasting. When they had finished the entire meal and were about to recite Grace and the Benediction after a wedding, he said to them, "Gentlemen, you have come to my house to recite the Benediction on the occasion of the

114

marriage of my son, but instead you must recite the prayer of consolation at the death of my son. You have come to lead him under the nuptial canopy, but instead you have to lead him to the grave."[1] Rabbi Zakkai, we are told, delivered the eulogy. Quoting Ecclesiastes, he said, "I said of laughter, 'it is mad,' and of mirth, 'what does it accomplish?' "[2]

Contained in this story are several lessons.

One has to do with the strength and courage of the father. When he saw his son dead he did not collapse, which would have been understandable. He did not disrupt the wedding feast to turn everybody's joy into sadness, which would have also been acceptable and understandable. No, he did not impose his own tragedy onto the lives of others. He kept, in silence, his own tragedy to himself.

Thus he showed a sense of balance and acceptance of the good and the bad, as if following in the steps of Job, who said, "shall we accept the good and not the bad?"[3] The father accepted with equanimity the joy of the wedding on the one hand and the sorrow of the death on the other, as if like a juggler, he held one on the right hand and the other on the left in a balancing act. He spoke to his guests in a calm, cool fashion. You come to marry. You come to bury. You come to a wedding. You come to a funeral. Both are facts of life. Both come and go. One is a continuation of life. One is a termination of life. When we marry, we initiate the process of procreation and the continuity of physical life. When we die, we initiate the process of spiritual life. A wedding and a funeral are both initiation rites, one into this world and the other into the next one. We come to one and end up at the other. The father of the groom understood that. He bided his time. At the right moment he invited his guests to the wedding and at the right time he invited them to the funeral too.

There are both grief and irony in the father's words. However, they are controlled, measured, and not excessive. There is an acceptance of the inevitable on the one hand and a display of structured, disciplined life on the other. Just as one recites prayers at a wedding, one must also recite prayers at a funeral. One must be cognizant of

---

1. *Midrash Rabbah, Kohelet* 2:4 and with slight variation in *Midrash Rabbah, Vayikra* 20:3.
2. Ecclesiastes 2:2.
3. Job 2:10.

God's presence at all times, be they happy or sad, good or bad. That is the ultimate test of faith. True faith is tested equally in times of trouble and in times of ease. Thus, the psalmist says, "To tell in the morning of Your kindness and Your faithfulness at night,"[4] which means, as my teacher Rabbi Dr. Abraham Kravetz, of blessed memory, once taught me, "when times are good [morning] we have to praise God for His kindness. When times are bad [night], we must, in spite of it, show our faith in God." That father who saw the joy of his son's wedding turn into the trauma of his son's funeral showed both appreciation of, and faith in, God.

Another lesson is Rabbi Zakkai's reaction. Rabbi Zakkai merely offered a commentary on the transience of time, the temporary existence of joy, and the madness of life itself. Looking at the extremes of the experiences of life into which one may be suddenly thrown, one can possibly go mad. I once had to officiate at a wedding. As I was about to get into the car to get there, I received an emergency call to rush to the hospital instead, for a congregant—a friend—was dying from a heart attack. He was being given shock treatment. It did not help. He died. I exchanged some words with the physicians and family. I said the right things, I hope, made my apologies, and drove off to the wedding. It was a house wedding. I walked into the house, with the picture of the dying man in my mind, and then standing in front of me were the nuptial canopy, the bride dressed in pure white, and the groom in his finest. They were both pupils of mine. I looked at them and the happy family and thought to myself, "What madness!"

Sane or mad, good or bad, sad or happy, life does not stop.

We acknowledge God at all times.

May we have the good fortune that our good times shall outweigh the bad ones and our fasts turn into feasts!

---

4. Psalms 92:3.

40

Start Living!

Sometimes one attends the funeral of someone who has lived a scrimpy life, saving everything for tomorrow, for a rainy day, for the future when there will be more time to enjoy the labor of his or her hands. That time, alas, has never come. The person suddenly dies, never having enjoyed the labor of his or her hands. Do you know such people? I, unfortunately, have had to bury many of them. There are also other people who never do the things in life they ought to have done, not because they had to save for tomorrow but because they were too busy at work. Day in, day out, from early dawn to late dusk they worked. They were too busy to spend time with family, relatives, and friends. They were too busy to be concerned with the affairs of the community. "When we retire," they tell you, "we'll have plenty of time for children, grandchildren, and the whole world." Unfortunately, the time to retire in this world never comes. Death has a priority. It strikes at the most inconvenient of times.

I am sure you know such people too. They are always too busy for themselves as well as for others. Now they have plenty of time but they are not here to use it. Then there are those who work only for their children. They deprive themselves of time, pleasure, comfort, and, often, health, working, saving, and bequeathing all their accumulated wealth to their children. However, then what happens? The children die before they do. The children forget their parents. The children squander their parents' inheritance, which they acquired with so much ease, but which their parents had accumulated with so much sweat and tears. Yes, you do know such people too. I know them. I buried them. I eulogized them. I comforted their survivors who not only mourned the loss of their parents but also bemoaned the fact that they "always worked so hard, they never had a chance to enjoy life." The mourners were grieving not only at the loss of their dear father or mother but also because all their life, in spite of what they had achieved, their works apparently were for naught. How true is this and how often does it happen?

Rabbi Samuel said to Rav Yehudah, "Oh, wise scholar! Do not delay your eating and postpone not your drinking, because this world in which we live is like a wedding." Rav said to Rav Hamnuna, "My son, if you have the means, enjoy yourself, because there is no pleasure in the grave, and death does not know about any tarrying, but should you say, 'I will leave a settlement to my children,' who will thank you for it in the grave? Men are like the grass of the field. Some blossom and others fade."[1]

This story covers it all. First, Rabbi Samuel tells us not to delay living life. The pursuit of worldly gain should not stop us from enjoying the labors of our hands now. In an age when all of us are conditioned to worry and plan for the material future, it is refreshing to hear a voice from the past telling us to enjoy life now, because, like a wedding, unless we enjoy it while it lasts, we will not have the chance to do so later. There is also another explanation of this statement. Rabbi Samuel tells his friend to enjoy the benefits of the material world quickly and get it over with in order to have time to pursue the lasting things in life, such as scholarship and the perfection of one's virtues, which last forever. Whichever view we take, both of them hold that one must never forget that life is fleeting. We should not delay living it to the fullest and in such a way that we are not distracted by the erroneous assumption that our opportunities to do things will last forever. Like a wedding feast, they, too, will pass. "Do not say, 'I will study when I have the free time,' " say the rabbis in another context, "for perhaps you will never be free."[2] Unless one lives and works now, one may never have the time to do so again.

---

1. *Eruvin* 54a (Vilna: The Widow and Brothers Romm, 1920).
2. *Avot* 2:4.

In like manner we are told that in the grave we cannot make up for the loss here. There, life is of a different dimension. In the grave, there is no pleasure as we know it. Therefore, enjoy life while you can, here and now, because if you do not, you may never have the chance. Death does not wait for you to finish your business. You must avail yourself of the chances you have now to live a meaningful life. Rav Hamnuna is talking not only about material means but also about one's intellectual and spiritual ability to see the real meaning of life.

That is why the story starts with the words, "Oh, wise scholar." It appeals to our wisdom and intellect, not to our appetite and passions – therefore the follow-up statement about leaving a "settlement" for one's children, which on the face of it seems to be a reasonable wish on the part of parents.

Unfortunately, in the grave, in the world to come, no one will thank us for that. We will be asked not "what have you left your children?" but "what have you done yourself?" We should not presume that because we give things to others we can be excused for not doing things for ourselves. Who can tell what will happen to our settlement? Maybe what we save they will squander. Like the grass of the field, "some blossom and others fade," so too are mankind's fortunes. Some of us prosper and some fail.

It can also be explained that Rav Hamnuna means this. He says, "How do you know whether your children's welfare depends on you? Maybe just like the grass of the field, which both blossoms and fades of its own accord without being planted or cared for, so, too, are men's fortunes on earth. When it is one's destiny to prosper, he will do so, in spite of circumstances and when it is his destiny to suffer, he will do so too, in spite of himself. Men are like the grass of the field."

Just as in life in general we ought to be mindful of these lessons, so, too, must we be mindful of these matters in times of bereavement in particular. During our life, we must not lose time by delaying what has to be done now for tomorrow or what we must enjoy ourselves by saying that we are leaving it for our children. So, too, must we not engage excessively in mourning and say that we are doing it for our parents or children, our brothers or sisters, our relatives or friends. When we mourn, we should mourn to express our own sorrow and sadness. We should express our own awareness of the limitations of life, which this death has suddenly brought to our attention. We should mourn our human destiny, which always ends in death, and then turn to the pursuit of life, because mourning for others will not excuse us for not living for ourselves. The death of our dear ones must not deprive us of carrying on life for ourselves. When they were alive, they had to live for themselves. Now, we, too, in spite of our loss of them, must continue to live for ourselves.

Cease mourning and start living!

41

The Wife of Your Youth

Not all deaths of a wife are the same. There is a difference in how a man responds to the death of a wife with whom he has lived or whom he knew for only a short while or whom he married in old age or for the second time and the death of a wife whom he knew from his youth and with whom he shared not only a marriage but also a lifetime. There is also a difference between a marriage that was a happy one and one that was not. It is possible to live with a person a lifetime and not even get to know that person; it is equally possible to live with a person for a short while that is more intense, joyous, and fulfilling than all the years of a lifetime. Yet there is no substitute for a marriage from the time of one's youth.

The rabbis teach us that Rabbi Samuel, son of Nachman, said, "For everything there is a replacement, except for the wife of one's youth."[1] Indeed, how does one find a replacement for one's youth? A lost youth is irreplaceable and so is one with whom we shared our youth.

The loss of the wife of one's youth is indeed a double loss. It means not only the loss of a partner in life but also the realization that one's own life has been taken away from him, because a wife from a man's youth is a reflection of his own past. Her departure is also a

---

1. *Sanhedrin* 22a.

departure of his own entire life. This is sad. What memories must pass before a man's mind at the loss of the wife of his youth? The hopes and dreams of childhood and adolescence. The carefree life of youth. The joys of spring and the pleasures of summer. The melancholy of autumn and the robustness of winter. The memory of the first child, the first job, the first house, a car, or a trip. The first family celebration. The marriage of the first child and the birth of the first grandchild and more and more, and then sickness in the family, death and sorrow among relatives, and now, finally, the breakup of the family tree, struck as by a bolt of lightning. Your tree has been split in half. Your partner in life is no more! This is cause for an endless mourning.

How do you find comfort when the wife of your youth and ipso facto your own youth have been taken away from you? You don't! You can only hope that the passage of time, the great healer of all wounds, will also heal your wound. Time, which kept you together, made you one, and now tore you apart, will also be the one to heal your wound.

"What time can do wisdom cannot accomplish"[2] we are taught. Time brought you together, giving you love and laughter and happiness and beauty. It gave you the chance to experience life in its fullness, good and bad. Now it took that gift away from you. You, though, still have time. You are alive. Give time a chance to heal your wound, to assuage the pain at the loss of the wife of your youth. Before, you had time to create memories. Now you have time to cherish them. Give time a chance to comfort you, and you shall be comforted.

---

2. *Chut Hashani* 112:2.

42

The Shortened Steps in Life

A wife is regarded in Jewish tradition as the guardian of a man's house and the sanctity of his family.[1] A man's material success in life, for example, is also ascribed to the credit of his wife.[2] She is the light of his life and the desire of his eyes.[3] The death of a wife was therefore always regarded as a most severe blow to her surviving husband. Her loss was compared in severity to the destruction of the Temple,[4] which is never to be forgotten and is to be continually mourned.

The rabbis had the greatest of sympathy and understanding for the man who lost a wife and offered him all the consolation and sympathy they could. Thus, "when a man's wife dies during his lifetime," Rabbi Yosi bar Chaninah, says, "his steps are cut short,"[5]

---

1. *Gittin* 52a, "A man's house is his wife," and *Shabbat* 118b. Said Rabbi Yosi, "I have never called my wife 'my wife' but I called her 'my house!' " See also *Midrash Rabbah Vayikra* 20:6; Abba Chanan says, "And he shall atone for himself and for his house . . ." (Leviticus 16:6, 11); his house means his wife.

2. *Baba Metzia* 59a. Rabbi Chelbo said, "A man should always be careful with the honor of his wife because his house is blessed only for the sake of his wife as it says Genesis 12:16, 'And Abraham prospered because of her.' "

3. The Rabbis in *Sanhedrin* 22a apply Ezekiel 24:16, "I am about to take away the delight of your eyes from you . . .," to a wife.

4. Ibid.

5. Ibid.

because, Scripture says, "the steps of his strength shall be straightened."[6] We see from this biblical verse that a wife is compared to a man's "strength." Thus, a wife is also the strength of a husband. She gives him courage and strength to face the task of life. When she is gone, his strength is gone and therefore his steps are cut short too. Rabbi Abahu said, "His counsel collapses,"[7] because it is written, "and his own counsel shall cast him down."[8] Again, the Bible refers to the wife as a "man's counsel," that is, his source of wit and wisdom. She is thus not only his source of physical strength but also his source of mental wisdom. Just as physical strength is symbolized by the stride of the feet, so too is mental wisdom expressed by the wit and counsel one shows in dealing with other people. A wife is a man's source of strength and wisdom.

When a man loses his wife, he loses his strength and his wisdom. His life becomes confined. His home is no longer the same, and neither is his life.

Indeed, we ask, how do you comfort such a man? You must tell him that it is all right to show his grief, to express his sorrow. We understand, we know how it feels. Perhaps in his knowledge that people understand and know what befell him when he lost his wife, he will find some comfort in it. "When the public shares in one's trouble it is of itself half a consolation."[9]

May all who mourn for their wife, and for their husband (for what we said about a wife is also true about a husband), find comfort in the knowledge that their sorrow is shared and in the faith that their heart's partner in life is with them in spirit and in love up in heaven as their partner was down here below on earth. He or she stands with the survivor as before.

May all who grieve for their husband or wife find comfort in these thoughts!

---

6. Job 18:7.

7. *Sanhedrin* 22a.

8. Job 18:7.

9. A popular Hebrew folk saying quoted by Even Kaspi in his commentary on Lamentations 2:13 (Vienna, 1853).

43

The Gift of Comfort

All death is tragic and sad. All mourners sustain a grievous loss when a mother or a father dies. All those who are bereaved need to be comforted. Yet some loss is easier to sustain and some mourners are easier to comfort. When does this take place? It happens when a man or woman dies in the fullness of his or her life, or even at a younger age, leaving behind a family of sons and daughters who are close to each other and who were also close to their father or mother who passed away. Such a family of mourners is much easier to comfort. I am sure you know such families. I have come across many of them.

Why is this so? Because somehow it appears to our naked eyes as well as to our intuitive grasp of reality that when a parent leaves children behind, especially children who identify with the family, then the dead has not been totally cut off from life. It is as though the departed continues to live, as though that life we feel was not wasted, as though that life continues, and as though the deceased has returned from life's journey through time and brought back wonderful gifts, the gifts of the surviving children, through whom the loved one continues to live.

Rabbi Pinchas, son of Chama, taught, "What does the verse 'and Hadad heard in Egypt that David slept with his fathers and Joab the captain of the host was dead'[1] mean? Why does Scripture use the word

---

1. I Kings 11:21.

125

'slept' when speaking of David, and 'dead' when speaking of Joab?" The answer, he says, is this: In the case of David, it is said that he "slept" because he left a son like himself. In the case of Joab, who did not leave a son like himself, it is said he was "dead."[2]

The moral of this story is quite obvious. According to the sage, the Bible does not regard death as the final act of one's existence on earth. A person may continue to live through children. Like David, those who leave children behind also remain behind after their physical remains depart. It can even be argued that such parents also continue to live, through the hereditary biological process, even in the physical sense, in their children. The physical presence, however, remains only if we can discern similarities in the physical likenesses of parents and children, which occur only as accidents of nature. The spiritual similarities of children and parents, on the other hand, are the results of conscious effort on the part of the survivors to follow in the steps of their father or mother. By preserving the qualities of life, personality, and character, that is, the values and standards, of their parents, children can retain the spiritual presence of their parents in this world. Thus, just as the survivors find sorrow in the departure and absence of their parents from this world, they also find comfort in the continual presence of their parents in their midst. They have no control over the physical departure of a father or a mother. They do, however, have control over the degree to which they want to follow in their parents' cherished footsteps. To the degree to which they do so, they will not only preserve their parents' spiritual presence but also find comfort and consolation in their own time of grief and sorrow.

Parents who die and leave children behind who are part of a well-knit and harmonious family have left their children not only the beautiful gift of family traditions but also the gift of comfort and consolation over their own departure!

---

2. *Baba Batra* 116a.

44

Life: The Passing Shadow

When is death most tragic and painful? When we think that life is most joyous and pleasurable. Indeed, the more we behold the goodness of life, the more death is an evil.

From infancy, we are told and taught to appreciate beauty – the beauty of the sky and the earth, the grandeur of the mountains and the serenity of the valleys, the sprouting grass and the greening trees, the falling white flakes of winter and the drizzling rain of summer, and even the falling leaves of autumn as well as the budding bushes of spring. Yes, all of these, in addition to the power and greatness of mankind's accomplishments, we are taught to admire and to regard as good. Our kindness to each other, our control over our own destiny, and the successful endeavors of individuals and nations alike are things we are taught are good. Indeed, "and God saw everything that He had made and, behold, it was very good."[1] Ever since then, mankind, too, has been looking at its work and finding it, in the main, "very good." Given this as our background, no wonder we crave life and regard death as an evil, and rightly so. However, is life really that good?

Thoughtful mankind, through the history of all civilizations, has looked upon life and found it sad, futile, and full of suffering. When we

---

1. Genesis 1:31.

127

see that "both the high and low perish, the rich and poor alike die,"[2] and
the mighty and the weak do not endure, what, then, is life, and what
value the struggle and the race to succeed and to gain fame, power, and
riches? Considering the suffering, the destruction, and the evil that roam
the world, it is no wonder that we develop a tragic sense of life.

"Who knows what is good for man in his life?"[3] asks Solomon.
"All the days of his futile life which he spends are like a shadow."

"Like what shadow?" ask the rabbis. "If like the shadow of a wall,
then there is some reality to it; if like the shadow of a palm tree, then
there is some reality to it, too."

David came and explained, "His days are like the shadow that
goes away."[4] Of course, this still does not explain the apparent problems the rabbis had in trying to define life. Indeed, what is wrong with
the shadow of a wall or a palm tree? The problem is that the rabbis are
looking for an example with no substance or reality to it, because they
know that that is what life is like. Therefore, the other examples are
not acceptable.

Rabbi Huna, in the name of Rav Acha, said, "It is like the bird
which flies and its shadow flies with it."

Samuel said, "It is like the shadow cast by flying bees, which has
no reality at all."[5] That is the point. Rav Acha's example of the flying
birds, though more ephemeral an example of reality than that expressed by the example of a wall or a palm tree, still has some
substance, and therefore reality, in it. Samuel therefore gives us the
example of the flying bees. The shadow they cast has no substance;
therefore it exemplifies the minimum degree of reality, thus approxi-
mating most closely the shadow cast by futile human life.

Human existence in and of itself is futile. It has no reality. It is here
today and gone tomorrow. In this world, human life is like the shadow
of flying bees.

However, even though the shadow of the bees in flight has no
reality, the bees themselves do. They create honey. They build bee-
hives. They pollinate the flowers and the trees. They do things in the
world.

---

2. Psalms 49:11.
3. Ecclesiastes 6:12.
4. Psalms 144:4.
5. *Kohelet Rabbah* 1:3.

Man's life may be like a shadow, but man's work is not. It creates, it does things, it improves the world.

When death strikes, one's shadow ceases to be – frail expression of reality that it was. However, one's work remains. We can take comfort that life in and of itself is short and futile and merely a shadow; therefore death is not the worst of things that can happen. We can take even greater comfort, though, in the knowledge that even though one's life comes to an end, one's work will endure forever!

45

The Loss of the Temple

Not all mourners feel the same pain from the same loss. Different people react differently to the loss of a wife, a husband, or a dear relative. We live in an age when many widowed people remarry, sometimes more than once. Is it possible that they should react to each death in the same manner? I know people who are happily remarried, yet make arrangements while still very much alive to be buried at death with their first partner, without any sensitivity for the feelings of the present partner; indeed, he or she stands by and smiles, as if it were a matter of routine practice. And indeed it is. Sometimes the surviving partner shows very little sorrow at the death of the second husband or wife, yet the same person fell apart when the first partner died. This may be true regardless of whether or not the first marriage lasted longer than the second one. It is indeed an accepted fact of life that one mourns severely the loss of a first partner in life. When we understand this and can show our understanding to the bereaved spouse, we will be able to console the more, and he or she will feel our sympathy the better.

Rabbi Yochanan said, "A man whose first wife died in his lifetime is as though the Temple was destroyed in his days."[1] One has to understand the meaning of the destruction of the Temple in the eyes of the Jews in order to fathom the depth of that statement and the

---

1. *Sanhedrin* 22a.

meaning of the loss of a wife. To the Jews the destruction of the Temple means unending sorrow and mourning. It is an event that is never forgotten. It is commemorated by praying and fasting every year. It serves as the epitome of personal and national mourning. It symbolizes the separation between God and the Jews and marks the beginning of the Jewish exile. The Temple stands for national pride, glory, splendor, and, most of all, communion with God. It cannot be replaced. It made the Jews special. Its loss can never be measured. One can never stop mourning over it.

Now then, this is also how the sages viewed the loss of one's first wife. Whatever is said about the meaning of the Temple to the Jews as a people must also be said about the meaning of the first wife to her husband. Whatever the Temple represented to the nation as a whole the first wife represented to her husband. Like the loss of the Temple, her loss, too, is irreplaceable. She cannot be forgotten. Like the mourning over the Temple, the mourning over her loss never stops. Without her, her husband is half the man she made him to be.[2] No wonder, then, that Rabbi Judah taught his son, Rabbi Isaac: "A man's spirit is quickened (that is, one finds pleasure in life) only with his first wife,[3] as it is written, 'Let your fountain be blessed and have joy of the wife of your youth.'[4] When he loses her, he also loses all his pleasures in life."

How do you comfort one who can never forget his loss? How do you comfort one who lost his very reason for existence? You can't.

The Jews found comfort at the loss of the Temple by talking about it, praying for its restoration, and remembering it on all posible occasions. You can be comforted in the loss of your first wife by talking about her, remembering her, and knowing that sometime, just as the Temple will be restored, so will you be restored, in heaven, to each other. This hope can give you strength to carry on while on earth. It can give you courage to face the reality of separation and loss. Hold on to her love and remember your life together. It will give you courage to face the future. Just as she was your helpmeet here on earth, she stands by you, up high in heaven, and sends you her blessings. Be blessed and comforted!

---

2. *Yevamot* 63a (Vilna: The Widow and Brothers Romm, 1920). Said Rabbi Elazar, "Any Jew who does not have a wife is not a man."

3. Ibid.

4. Proverbs 5:18.

46

Knocking at the Door

The confrontation with death constitutes not only a moment of bereavement and sorrow but also one of contemplation and reflection about the value, meaning, and purpose of life. I realize that when one is in mourning and one's heart is bleeding, it is not the time to philosophize, yet we have all experienced instances when we hear well-meaning friends try to comfort the bereaved by saying, "Now try to be philosophical about it. After all, she was . . . or he was. . . . It was a blessing in disguise." Indeed, perhaps this is the best thing to say at the moment, when there is nothing else to say, trite though it might sound.

There is an account in the Talmud about a debate that took place some two thousand years ago between two major schools of thought. They were the House of Shammai and the House of Hillel. They debated the question of whether it was good for man to have been created or not. The debate lasted for two and a half years. The House of Shammai argued, "It would have been better for man not to have been created altogether than to have been created." The House of Hillel argued, "It is better for man to have been created than not to have been created." Finally, they voted on the issue and reached the conclusion, "It would have been better for man not to have been created altogether than to have been created. However, since he has already been created, let him investigate his past doings." Others say, "he should examine what he is presently doing."[1]

We learn three important lessons from this story.

1. All in all, after careful evaluation of the lot of mankind, when all is said and done, no matter what we accomplish, the fact is that we die. Death conquers all. Based on the ultimate end of life on this earth, our lot is hopeless. Death, not life, is king. And so, had we had a chance of being or not being created so as to live a life under such circumstances, we all would have presumably chosen not to be created. This, however, is not for us to decide. The fact is, the rabbis recognized, that we are here. The questions therefore facing us are, Now what? Where do we go from here? What do we do about it? Their answers bring us to the second lesson.

2. At the end of our life, we must give an account of ourselves. Therefore, we should examine what we did all through our years on earth. What kind of person were we? What kind of work did we perform? How did we use our time? How did we relate to ourself, family, friends, business, society, country, and so on? At the end of our life, the answers to these questions will determine what we are and what our creation was all about. Since we never know when our end will be, we must live so that every day we are ready to say good-bye and every day we should be able to give an accounting of ourselves and the work we did.

Benjamin Franklin, in his autobiography, writes that every night, before he went to bed, he would prepare a list of things to do the next day. The items were things that would build his character and develop his personality traits. Naturally there were virtues to be followed and vices to be avoided. At the same time, he would also check off his performance on the day that had just ended. If he missed out on some virtue or action, he would make a point to be sure to do it the next day.[2] The same applies also to us. Each day may be our last one. When the sun sets, we should review our daily work and investigate our performance carefully. It may be our last chance. The results of these investigations may be the sum total of the meaning of our life and the reason why we were created.

1. *Eruvin* 13b.

2. Benjamin Franklin, *His Life as He Wrote It*, ed. Esmond Wright (Cambridge, MA: Harvard University Press, 1989), p. 82.

3. The third lesson the rabbis teach us is not to look at our past performances. They are beyond our control now. Instead, we should examine our immediate and present actions. Indeed, we should act carefully and thoughtfully at all times. We should not dwell on the past but concentrate on the present. Life is too unpredictable and too short to dwell on the past, which we no longer can control. We should rather pay attention to the deeds we do right now. If we dwell on the past, we become petrified and bitter like Lot's wife, who, because she stopped and looked back instead of forward, turned into salt.[3]

The truth is that both approaches to life are correct. That is why the Talmud records them both. We must examine carefully our past deeds in order not to repeat our mistakes and in order to reinforce our good traits, and we must be careful about what we are doing now so as not to commit any bad acts now, which we will have to correct tomorrow.

At the end of the day, when death strikes at our door and we lose a dear one, be it a mother or father, a husband or wife, a son or daughter, a lover or friend, or a neighbor or associate, we are struck as well by the realization of the futility of life. However, there is not much we can do about it. We are here. We have been created, futility or no futility. We cannot escape the fact that we are alive. Now, therefore, just as we must accept our creation as a fact, we must also accept our destruction as a fact. "Man is born in spite of himself, and man dies in spite of himself" proclaims the Yom Kippur Prayer Book.[4] The question is not whether this is good or bad. This is now a theoretical issue only. The real question is, What do we do about it? The answer is obviously to make the most of our life. Check carefully what you did yesterday. Be careful what you are doing today. What you did and are doing are both what you are and what you will be after your journey's end.

When death comes, receive it philosophically. It began to knock at the door of your dear one whom you are now mourning the

---

3. Genesis 19:26.

4. *Avot* 2:29. See also the Yom Kippur Service, *The High Holy Day Prayer Book*, trans. Philip Birnbaum (New York: Hebrew Publishing Co., 1979), where we read, "Man comes from dust and ends in dust" (p. 794), and, "They die by Thy decree and are revived by Thy mercy" (p. 790).

moment he or she was born. Your dear one died now only because it took that long for him or her to open the door. Remember, too, that death is knocking at your door as well from the moment you were born. At the right moment, you, too, will open the door. It happens to all of us, one way or another. The point is, when the time comes, do we open the door gracefully or not?

47

Man's Companions

What is the sum total of one's life on earth? When we die, what do we leave behind by which we are to be remembered? Shall we be remembered by the wealth we left our family? The life of luxury or poverty we led while here on earth? The work we did in our profession? The answers to these questions are important because they will provide us with comfort and consolation at the loss that we sustain when one of our dear parents, brothers or sisters, or relatives or friends dies, leaving us bereft of his or her company and fellowship. Will we find comfort in the memory of our loved one's good work in the office or in the factory? What is it that is really important? In short, what is the best bequest one can leave one's family and friends that will comfort them? To put it in other words, in what can the bereaved find comfort?

The masters teach us that "When a man departs from this world he is accompanied neither by silver nor gold, neither by precious stones nor pearls, but only by the Torah and his good deeds, for Scripture says, 'when you walk it will lead you, when you lie down it will watch over you, and when you are awake it will talk with you.'[1] 'When you walk it will lead you' means in this world; 'when you lie down it will watch over you' means in the grave; and 'when

---

1. Proverbs 6:22.

you are awake it will talk with you' means in the world of the future."[2]

We learn from this statement several lessons not only about what happens to the dead but also what kind of life one ought to lead, and it is this, the quality of one's life here on earth, that determines what will happen to us, and ipso facto, in what those who mourn us might find consolation.

1. We learn that there are three stages to reality. The first stage consists of our present existence on earth; the second stage is in the grave after we die, when the body is interred and disintegrates and the soul continues to exist in heaven; and, finally, the third stage is the time when the dead are resurrected and the soul and body reunited and restored to life again.

2. There are two areas of human pursuit that are always there to help us and stand by us. These are the pursuit of Torah study or the study of those disciples that provide us with the proper insight into the nature of life and what is proper human conduct on the one hand and the performance of good deeds, meaning, leading a life that is helpful to our fellows and to society as well as not damaging to ourselves on the other.

3. The results of one's accomplishments in these two areas of human endeavor are superior to all other human activities. They endure forever. They are always *good*. They transcend all the barriers that separate one form of reality from another. They are eternal and equally good in this world, in the world of the spirit after we die, and in the world of the future after our resurrection. All else may change, but the nature of the life we lead on earth remains forever ours. It is our fingerprint and our voiceprint on eternity. No matter where we are, what we do, or what we become, these remain the same. The deeds we do are us, but among the deeds we do, only those of intellectual pursuit, exemplified by the study of the Torah and the performance of good deeds matter. Only they remain. They are our record of the sum total of our existence in this world, the world of the grave (and the heavens) and the world of the future. This is what we are. If we lead a life in which we do our very best in these areas, then these, our actions in life, will stand

---

2. *Avot* 6:9.

by us both in this world and in the other two worlds. That is all
that really matters after all!

If your dearly departed lived a life that matched or approximated these
standards, if he did his best to know what is life and how to conduct
himself accordingly, if he did no harm to himself, if he helped fellow
neighbors and benefited society – if that is the bequest that is left you,
you can be sure that these deeds of his are standing by him now in
heaven and that they will stand by him equally well in the world of the
future, even as they stood by him and molded his life and personality
here on earth. This is the finest legacy he could have left you: the
knowledge that he continues to live even now and will someday come
back to life because of the life he led when he was here. Find comfort in
the fact that his life on earth was not in vain. It continues forever and
ever. Someday, at the right time, you shall all be together again!

48

Bend Your Head

What are the enduring personality traits that last forever? Are they physical? Surely not, for those disintegrate with the body. Are they our ideas and our thoughts? Maybe, but thoughts remain within us and disappear with our departure from the world. We mean those traits that are responsible for our development on the one hand and our self-expression in our relationships with our fellows on the other. We are talking about behavioral characteristics, which identify us in the minds and eyes of others and by which we shall always be remembered.

The rabbis put these questions differently. They asked, "What kind of person has a share in the world of the future?"[1] That is, who is assured of surviving beyond death because of achievement here on earth? They tell this story.

A message was sent from the scholars of Palestine to those of Babylonia, asking, "Who is the man that has a share in the world to come?" The answer was, "He who is meek, humble, bends his head when entering and leaving the house, always studies the Torah without claiming any credit for it!"[2] What do all these traits mean? Says one of the great scholars,[3] there are people who pride themselves on their

---

1. *Sanhedrin* 88b.
2. Ibid.
3. Maharsha—Shmuel Eliezer ben Yehudah Ha-levi Edels, *Rosh Yeshivah* and commentator on the Talmud (b. Posen 1555, d. Wallen, Austria, 1631).

knowledge and wisdom, and there are those who pride themselves on their own bodily appearance and physical prowess, and there are still others who pride themselves on their wealth. Therefore, we are told that those who will have a share in the world to come humble themselves in all of these areas. Thus, "a meek man" is meek about his own knowledge and wisdom; a "humble" man means a man who is "humble" about his physical power; one who "bends his head" refers to his humility about his wealth. It means that he does not flaunt riches or a beautiful and stately-looking house, as is sometimes the custom among the rich. "He always studies" means that after having acquired all these characteristics of humility, this man also has the virtue of studying . . . and "without claiming any credit" means studying beyond the required limits yet not boasting about it, saying "even though I fulfil my duty by setting aside time to study, I also study morning and evening."[4]

We may learn from this the important lesson that in order to acquire eternity we do not have to shun the physical world, negate our bodily existence, avoid commerce and the pursuit of riches and the comfort of material life, or merely do our duty in the pursuit of knowledge. No, that is not required of us. What we are told is the opposite. Indeed, do pursue knowledge and wisdom; do engage in the acquisition of wealth; do build up your physical strength; do study beyond your required duty, but when you do all of these things, remember, do not be proud of your own achievements; do not boast about yourself; do not flaunt your possessions. Do not let it go to your head. Remember that you are not going to live forever. There is still a limit to your achievements and your ability, both mental and physical. Death will still have your worldly goods. Be meek. Be humble. Bend your knee. Study more. Doing all of these, one will have a share in the world to come! Really, when you stop to think about it, the road to eternity is not that difficult. All it calls for is to bend your head a little bit!

Who knows a person better than his or her immediate family—the father, the mother, the wife, the husband, the children? You who read this know your dearly departed better than others. You know how he measured up to these standards. The more he did, the surer you can be that he is now enjoying a share in the world to come. He exists there, and, being there, he continues to be here, too, with you, in spirit and in love.

Take heart! Be comforted!

---

4. Maharsha—*Chidushei Halachot Va'agadot* on *Sanhedrin* 88b.

49

A Good Name

Death is the great equalizer. It makes no distinction. It gathers in everyone. "The great and the small are both there."[1] The angel of death does not discriminate. When the time comes to smite, death does not differentiate between people or between places, between young or old, healthy or sick, mighty or weak, rich or poor, prince or plebeian, be it in the skies or under the seas, on the land or on the waters, on the mountaintops or in the valley depths. When death is out to bring you home, the mission is sure to succeed. Death equalizes not only all people but also all living creatures. Beast and human become one. "The advantage of human over beast is none."[2] What, then, is the difference, indeed, between humans and animals if at the end of their lives they are both equally dead? What a sorry state!

The Talmud[3] tells that when Rabbi Yochanan concluded the study of the Book of Job, he said, "The end of man is to die, and the end of cattle is to be slaughtered and everything is destined to die. Happy is the man who was reared in the study of the Law and who toils in the Law and acts in such a manner that brings pleasure to his Creator and has grown up with a good name and departed this world with a good

---

1. Job 3:19.
2. Ecclesiastes 3:19.
3. *Berachot* 17a.

name." About such a man, Solomon said, "A good name is better than precious oil, and the day of death than the day of one's birth."[4]

Indeed, the difference between human and beast is in the good name one acquires in this world and the work one does in studying the Law. Not only does this differentiate human from beast but also person from person. One who acquires a reputation for studying the Law is also one who acquires a good name. A good name lasts forever. A reputation is a legacy. Not in vain do people say that it is hard to live down a bad reputation. Similarly it is hard to erase a good name. The person who has a good name earned it by a certain lifestyle and hard work. One who has a good name among one's fellows also has a good name with his Maker. Such a one will be remembered not only here on earth but also high up in heaven.

You can rest assured that your dear one lives on. Your dear one's good name will preserve him or her here on earth and there in heaven.

Take comfort. Your dear one left you a good name!

---

4. Ecclesiastes 7:1.

50

He Took Nothing

There are people who are blessed with many years, a good family, a job, and a good life, yet when they die they go quietly. Nobody pays much attention to their disappearance. It is as though their life and their death made no difference. The survivors take their loss in their stride. They go through the motions of mourning and return quickly to their tasks at hand, of making a living and surviving. You come to such a house of bereavement and you don't know whom to comfort – the living or the dead. It is sad to see a human being go from this world and not be missed. What was the meaning of the person's life? Indeed, how do we comfort the memory?

There is a lesson taught in the name of Rabbi Meir who lived some two thousand years ago. This is what he taught.[1]

When man enters this world his hands are clenched in a fist, as if to say, "The whole world is mine, I shall possess it!" When he departs from this world, his hands are straight and open, as if to say, "I have possessed nothing of this world." Thus, Solomon says, "As he came out naked from his mother's womb, so shall he return naked. He shall take nothing for his labor, which he can carry away in his hand."[2] How totally true.

---

1. *Midrash Rabbah, Kohelet* 5:21.
2. Ecclesiastes 5:14.

We come into this world hoping, planning, and looking forward to possessing it. In our youth we think we can conquer mountains. We are out to get and to enjoy the world. We are reaching out for everything and anything with our hands, closing our fist around it and grabbing it for ourselves. Albert Einstein once observed that in his day and age, young people had no idealism. They are out only to see what they can get out of the world. They are out to gratify and enjoy their material needs.[3] This may have been true not only of the young people in his time but of all people all the time. Only at death do we realize that no matter how strongly and frequently we reached out to get hold of the world around us, at the end of the day when we are laid to eternal rest, our hands are stretched and straight. We have nothing to show for all our hustle and bustle. All our hard work did not bring us anything. We come in alone and we depart alone.

The one who dies and takes nothing along can take comfort by not being alone in this. This is the state of mankind. We cannot take with us our worldly possessions any more than we can preserve our own physical existence.

Survivors who take the loss of a dear one as if it were a casual occurrence are akin to one's physical possessions. One should not expect them to show grief and bereavement where none was forthcoming. It is their loss. Perhaps they had only a biological kinship. They missed out on the spiritual, emotional, and human attachment that usually bind a family together. The one who is dead should, however, be comforted. His or her lot in life was similar to all mortals, who, like all who are born, had a mission, if only to beget a new generation of people. To do that is also an accomplishment. It is part of one's reaching out to the physical world. We think of it also as possessions. Such possessions, however, cannot be taken to the grave. They are left behind. The one who died also took nothing along from this world but left behind instead, however, a little bit of self, if only in the biological sense. Such a piece of humanity will continue in this world while the departed is returning to the world above. Such a soul will rest in peace!

---

3. I heard this from David Ben-Gurion, who told it to me on the first night of Chanukah in 1970.

51

Praise Them!

Should we say this world is bad just because we, in the end, die? Does our death negate the beauty of nature or its awesomeness, splendor, and grandeur? Who can stand in the presence of lofty mountains with their snowcapped tops touching the sky or their spearlike peaks piercing the heavens and not be awed? Who can look down into a green valley or see a rushing river and not be amazed at the marvels of nature? Who can stand at the seashore watching a sunset and not be moved or raise eyes to the mountains in the morning and not be touched as the burning ball of fire bursts into the sky? What about the beauty of all of God's creatures – the beasts in the forests and the animals on the farm? Aren't they something to behold? What is more beautiful than a cow nursing its little calf or a horse racing down the meadow? What is more slick than a leopard giving chase to the prey or more fearsome than a lion's roar? What about man? Isn't he beautiful? Just look at him in all his extremes: tall and short, fat or skinny, black or white, blue- or brown-eyed, perfectly shaped and almost as perfect in deformity? Oh, what of man? Yes, and what about all that he has created? Is it not something to praise and proclaim? Can we say that death makes nothing out of it? Is death the end of all? Surely there must be more to life. It cannot die with our physical death.

A wise man called Geniba explained the verse in Ecclesiastes "Just

145

as man came out of his mother's womb naked, so shall he go back as he came"[1] by telling the following parable.

"This verse may be understood through the story of the fox who came upon a vineyard that was fenced in on all sides. The fox wanted to enter it but could find only one small hole through which he could do so. However, the hole was too small for him to pass through, so he fasted for three days and lost enough weight to go through the hole. Once inside the vineyard, he feasted to his heart's content. He partook of and enjoyed everything he could find there and became fat again. When he wanted to leave the vineyard, he came to the same hole, but lo and behold, he could not go through it. He was too fat. So, again he fasted for three days and lost all the fat he gained, and became lean and slender once more, in order to go through the hole. When he got out of the hole and was on the other side of the vineyard, he turned around, looked at it, and said, 'Vineyard, vineyard, how good are you, and how good is the fruit that you contain! Everything you have is beautiful and praiseworthy! However, what benefit can one derive from you? Just as one enters you, so must one leave you!'

"Thus," concluded Geniba, "it is also with this world."[2]

Indeed, so it is. The world, like the vineyard, is praiseworthy. Everything in it is also beautiful. Unfortunately we cannot take it with us when the time comes for us to go, yet that does not change anything. The world remains as ever, beautiful. Indeed, because of man's works it may become even better. Unlike the fox in the vineyard, man does not merely enjoy the fruits of the world, but he also improves upon them. Even though when he departs he takes nothing of it with him, he nevertheless leaves something of himself behind in the world for others to come to and to enjoy. This is the difference between a fox and a man.

However, other wise men differ with this approach to the meaning of this verse of Ecclesiastes. They maintain it teaches us another lesson: that man departs this world in the same manner as he comes.[3]

"He comes into this world noisily and he departs noisily. He

---

1. Ecclesiastes 5:4.

2. *Midrash Rabbah, Kohelet* 5:21. See also the commentary on same by *Matnot Kehunah.*

3. Ibid.

comes into the world crying and he departs crying."[4] That is, when he is born, he cries because he does not want to depart from the comfort, warmth, and care of the womb and enter into the cold, threatening, and unknown world. When he is about to die, he does not want to leave the world and all the goodness therein and go to the unknown yonder.[5] "He comes into this world with affection and departs it with affection,"[6] the rabbis comment. That is, when he is born, everybody hugs him, kisses him, plays with him and loves him. When he dies, everybody shows affection, love, and care for him. They all profess their love of him and how much they miss him.[7] Some say that "he is born in spite of himself and he dies in spite of himself."[8] That is, man prefers not to be born, just as later on he prefers not to die, but in both instances he has no control over his destiny. So, "He comes into this world with trepidation and leaves this world with trepidation." "He comes into the world with a sigh and departs this world with a sigh."[9] That is, he regrets having to leave the world of the womb as well as the world of the living. Indeed both departures are painful to him. "He is without knowledge when he is born, and he is without knowledge when he dies."[10] That means, at birth he has no knowledge of things to come and when he becomes old, he also loses his faculty of knowledge of things past.[11]

According to all of these interpretations, we can see that the sages maintain that indeed, the world of the soul, prior to birth, and the world of the body, after birth, are both good.[12] Man is comfortable and

---

4. Ibid.

5. *Anaf Yosef* on ibid.

6. Ibid. The *Matnot Kehunah*, op. cit., points out that the righteous are happy to depart from this world because of the suffering here, and the *Eitz Yosef*, ibid., adds that they are happy to depart this world because of the light and bliss that await them in the next world.

7. Ibid. See also *Eitz Yosef*, op. cit., on same, who says that these are tears of joy, namely that the soul is happy to come into this world and happy to return to its source because of the suffering that one goes through at the time of death (or in life in general).

8. Ibid.

9. Ibid. See also *Midrash Tanchuma*, Exodus, on *Parshat Pekudei*, chap. 3, for a discussion of this topic.

10. See n. 7.

11. *Midrash Tanchuma*, op. cit.

12. *Nidah* 30b: "A man has no better time than the time when he is in his mother's womb."

happy in both of them. If it were up to him, he would remain where he is but that is out of his control. This, however, should not in any way diminish our appreciation of the goodness and beauty of this world. If anything, it teaches us to hold in greater esteem and to value more our life in this world – both the physical and social world in which we were privileged to live.

Do not grieve for the dead. Praise them.

Praise them for having been part of this beautiful and good universe.

Praise them for having been part of the social order.

Praise them for having been given the privilege to have been born in the first place.

Praise them for having been a life.

Praise them for having been part of you.

Praise them for having been your friend.

Praise them for having brought you into the world.

Praise their lives, and in that praise find comfort for the sorrow and grief you suffer at your loss!

52

All Gifts Must Be Returned

Even though in the hour of grief our mind leaves us and our heart takes possession of our entire being, nevertheless, I want to appeal to your mind.

Perhaps in this way I will reach your soul, if not your mind, and bring you a little bit of consolation and comfort in this trying moment of your life. I always find wisdom in the deeds and words of wise men and women, and, in applying their experiences to our life, I find succor. There was some nineteen hundred years ago a husband and a wife. He was called Rabbi Meir and she, Beruriah. He was a renowned scholar and sage, she a wise and greatly respected woman. They had two sons, young, handsome, and promising.

One *Shabbat* afternoon when Rabbi Meir was lecturing in the academy, both sons suddenly died.[1] The mother reacted with grief and sorrow. Her heart was broken, but even as she wept for her two sons she was also very worried about her husband. She wanted to spare him his heartache and pain, which she feared would be even greater

---

1. *Midrash Mishlei*. (Vilna: The Widow and Brothers Romm, 1892); reprinted in Jerusalem, (1964), ed. Shlomo Baber, pp. 108–109. Proverbs 31:10. See also *Sefer Yalkut Hameiri Al Mishlei*, ed. Elazar Halevi (Jerusalem: Grünhoot, 1891) and *Yalkut Shimoni, Midrash Al Torah Nevi'im Uketuvim*, part two, *Nevi'im Rishonim Va'acharonim* (Jerusalem, 1959), p. 1,002, col. 2. (There are minor textual differences among the three printings.)

than hers, because she knew the great love between father and sons. So she devised a plan on how to break the sad news to her husband when he came home from the academy. She took the bodies of her sons and placed them next to each other on the bed in one of their bedrooms and covered them appropriately. When at the conclusion of the Sabbath her husband came home, he asked his wife, "Where are my two sons?" the following dialogue ensued.

"They went to the academy," she replied.

"I looked for them at the academy and I did not see them there," he said. In the meantime, Beruriah gave him wine to make *Havdalah*.[2] He recited the *Havdalah* prayers. Again he asked, "Where are my two sons?"

"They went somewhere and will soon return," she told him and served him dinner. When he finished reciting the Grace Prayer, she said to him, "My master, I have a question to ask of you."

"Ask," came the response.

"Recently a man came and gave me something to watch and now he came to take it back. Should I return it to him or not?"

Said he to her, "My child,[3] whoever has been entrusted with something must return it to its owner!"

She then said to him, "My master, if it were not for what you have just said to me I would not have returned it to him." What did she then do? She took him by the hand and led him to the room where their sons were lying, brought him to the bed, and removed the cover from the bodies of their sons.

Rabbi Meir saw his two dead sons lying on the bed and began to cry and exclaim, "My sons, my sons! My teachers, my teachers! My sons because you showed me the respect due a father, my teachers because you have enlightened me with the teaching of your Torah wisdom!"

At that moment Beruriah said to Rabbi Meir, "My master, didn't you tell me that I must return to its master that which was entrusted to me?"

---

2. *Havdalah* means, literally, separation. It is the name of the ceremony marking the end of the Sabbath day and the beginning of the six days of the week designed for work. The ceremony consists of reciting a blessing over a cup of wine, spices, and a candle with no less than two wicks. It parallels the Kiddush ceremony ushering in the Sabbath.

3. In our text, the two word used is *"biti"*—my daughter. In either case, it is an expression of endearment.

Whereupon the rabbi said, "The Lord gave and the Lord has taken away. Blessed be the name of the Lord" (Job 1:21).

The following rounds off this story with a pointed and poignant observation.

Rabbi Chaninah, it tells us, said, "With these words she (Beruriah) comforted her husband and he had peace of mind. Therefore, it says. 'A woman of valor who can find' (Proverbs 31:10)."

Indeed, what a woman of valor she must have been to muster up the self-control needed to help her husband and to face and overcome her own grief as a mother. What a marvel of a woman!

My dear friends, all life is a gift. Our own life is a gift to ourselves. We are a gift to our parents, even as our children are a gift to us. All gifts must be returned. The One who is the Creator of life is also the Giver of life. He alone determines for how long we may keep the gift He grants us. When the time comes, we must return it. It is not ours to keep, only to make the most of it. This is true of all life. Therefore, let us remember the moments that we enjoyed it. Let us cherish the memories when we shared the gift of life with our loved ones.

The life of your dear children, parents, brother, sister, husband, or wife as well as that of your friends was given to you in trust, trusts to which you became accustomed and which gave you happiness and brought you meaning and purpose in life. Enjoy the thoughts about all the pleasures your dear ones brought–the times and dreams you shared. Be thankful you have so many good things to remember. Think deeply and they will come to mind. Beruriah understood what it meant to appreciate the good fortune of being a trustee of life and the treasurer of dear ones, but she also knew that all gifts must be returned. Her husband had taught her that and so he, too, accepted the inevitability of parting.

I hope you, too, will realize that your dear ones were God's gifts to you and that now you have to let go. May you find comfort in your memories!

53

Blessed Shalt Thou Be

When all is said and done and we have to face the ultimate reality of accepting the loss of a dearly beloved member of the family, a friend, or an acquaintance and look the inevitable straight in the eye, grit our teeth in pain, clench our fists in sorrow and recognize in frustration our limitations and our powerlessness over life, we ask the question, "Now what?" Do we stop here and stare into the void or do we take it a step further, asking what was the meaning of all this – how did the departed one affect our life; indeed, what kind of a person was he or she – and take comfort from that very life?

To answer the questions, I would like you to turn with me to a passage of the Talmud and its teaching of what the Bible means when it blesses us. Perhaps the one we mourn was such a blessed individual whose lifestyle shall therefore provide us with an answer to the question of how to measure the loss of a dear one.

It is written, "Blessed shalt thou be when thou comest in and blessed shalt thou be when thou goest out."[1] The sages are puzzled. Surely it should be written in reverse, for one should be first blessed when one "goes out," then when one "comes in." Therefore, they say the verse teaches us something special. When it speaks about our "coming in," it means our coming into the world, and by "going out"

---

1. Deuteronomy 28:6.

it means our going out of the world.[2] That is, one should be born free
of sin and die without having sinned. Commenting upon this, Rabbi
Berachiah says it is written, "There is a time to be born and a time to
die."[3]

We in turn ask, "Surely we know that there is a time when one is
born and when one dies. What, then, is the purpose of this verse?" It
lets us know that happy is the one whose time of death is as good as the
time of birth. Just as one was pure when one was born, so should one
be pure when one dies. Therefore, it is written, "Blessed shalt thou be
when thou comest in and blessed shalt thou be when thou goest out."[4]

How wonderful it must be for the survivors to be able to say, "All
his years that person lived a pure life, just as when first born." Indeed,
what is the nature of a newborn? A newly born child brings joy to its
parents and happiness to the family. It hasn't harmed anyone. It is full
of promise. It looks at the world with awe. Everything it sees it marvels
at. It knows only love. It senses its own vulnerability, frailty, and
dependence on parents. It is outgoing and friendly. It is innocent. If
only we could preserve these qualities as we grow older. If your dearly
beloved departed this world with some measure of those childhood
qualities, able to retain a little bit of the purity of life with which he or
she came into this world and to depart from it in the same way, in spite
of all the vicissitudes and temptations of life, then indeed your dear
departed one was blessed, not only on coming in but also on going out.

Be comforted in your knowledge of all of those pure deeds and
that good life!

---

2. *Baba Metzia* 107a.

3. Ecclesiastes 3:2.

4. *Midrash Rabbah* on the Torah and Five Scrolls, Deuteronomy 7:5 (Vilna: The
Widow and Brothers Romm, 1896), Deuteronomy, p. 76.

54

In the Fullness of Life

I know it is hard to grasp why a person should be cut off in the prime of life, when so much still remains to be done, when there is so much to look forward to: joy from children growing up, a business prospering, a career just developing, and life just beginning to show the promise of the rewards for hard work. Yet such is life that when one is struck down, all of this is left, as if nothing had ever been there. But this is not true, because there are people, relatives, and friends who are left behind, asking why? Why him? Why her? There is a job crying out: "Who will finish the work?"

We all assume that life has a beginning, a middle, and an ending. That is true. The only problem is that, although we can identify the beginning, we seldom know when the middle occurs or when the end is to be. "A man's life is three score years and ten"[1] the psalmist tells us. But what does that mean? Does it mean that every person should live to the age of seventy years? And if so, what do we mean by a year? Do we mean the accumulation of days, weeks, months, and years – in short, the passage of time – or do we mean the amount of work, creativity, achievement at our job, play, and the life both private and public that one has managed to compress in the course of that time? If so, it becomes relative, does it not? Some people are late starters; others

---

1. Psalms 90:10.

are early bloomers. Some work at whatever they do quickly; others, slowly. In short, one can live three score years and ten and accomplish no more than another could in thirty-five, whereas still another can accomplish in thirty what another would take a lifetime to do. It is not therefore how long we live but how well we live and how wisely and productively we use our time, which counts.

"One person may acquire the entire world to come in one hour."[2] Indeed, it is possible to achieve immortality with one sublime act. It could be physical or moral courage. "And one person may acquire the entire world in several years."[3] Just as people are different, so are their activities and levels of achievement. It could be a stroke of genius or an act of kindness. There are people who live a hundred years and end up in oblivion just the same. The question is not how long one lived but how well.

"It is not your job to complete your work,"[4] Rabbi Tarfon teaches. "Nevertheless," he continues, "neither are you free to turn away from it."[5] One is born to do a job in the world. One's duty is to do it well, not to finish it. No one can finish it. Life only continues. We can only move, push, or guide it along by giving it a stir in the right direction, so that we make it easier for others who come after us to do their job. Who can tell when our job is done? We only know that we have to do it. Perhaps in the course of thirty years we have done as much as the one who lived "three score years and ten." Who knows when the middle and the end of our life occur in the line of continuous life? We can judge only how well we did what we were entrusted to do. Your loved one who has been taken in the prime of life lived a full, creative life. It was not a duty to finish a job, nor was your dear one free to leave it, but it was the duty to do the job and do it well. This was done, which is why there was so much more for the departed to look forward to. Now it is up to you to continue that work by following in his or her footsteps and making your dear one's memory as proud of you as you are of the dear one.

---

2. *Avodah Zarah*10b (Vilna: The Widow and Brothers Romm, 1920).

3. Ibid.

4. *Avot.* Part of same volume as *Avodah Zarah* (Vilna: The Widow and Brothers Romm, 1920), chap. 2:16, p. 86.

5. Ibid.

55

Choose Life!

One of the most, if not the most, famous and well-known prayers among the Jewish people is the *Kaddish,* commonly known as the Mourner's Prayer. The Hebrew word *Kaddish* means sanctification. It is recited by mourners at the funeral of a dear one, – a father, a mother, a child, a brother, or a sister. It is a mandatory prayer, to be recited by the survivors of those relatives.[1] It is also recited during the Week of Mourning at the home of the mourners[2] and it continues to be recited by them for eleven months after the funeral.[3] In addition, it is recited each year on the anniversary of the death of a parent and of other immediate relatives.[4] Yet the entire prayer does not contain a single reference or allusion to death or bereavement. It is in its entirety a hymn of praise of God. It is an expression of our sense of awe, reverence, exaltation, and veneration of God and His grandeur, manifestation in, and rule over the world. In short, it is our sanctification of God. The question therefore arises, Why is this prayer recited at a house of mourning?

---

1. *Yoreh Dei'ah,* part three (New York: *Otzar Halacha,* 1959); *Hilchot Aveilut* 376:4, p. 30. See especially the *Ramah* (Rabbi Moshe Isserles) on this section.

2. Ibid.

3. Ibid.

4. *Ramah,* ibid.

Indeed, nothing could be more paradoxical than to speak of God, the source of life, in a house of mourning, the place of death. The two are mutually exclusive.

The very nature of our dilemma provides us with the solution.

It is understandable that at a time of bereavement, mourning, loss, separation, and death one should feel withdrawn from life. The very nature of the Jewish way of mourning, which calls upon the bereaved to stay put at home, sit on low stools, and not go outdoors except in an emergency, is not only a form of withdrawal from life itself but also a way of identification with the departed himself or herself. Even more than that, during that period of loss and trauma, it is quite natural to feel anger, frustration, pain, and hurt and to turn against God. In fact, at times of mourning, many who are bereaved raise very painful and sharp questions about God. It is understandable that they do. Job is famous for venting his anger at God and questioning Him about righteousness, suffering, and evil. Most of all, Job expresses the anguished question that is reechoed on the lips of almost all mourners: "Why?"[5]

Failing to receive a reply, some people turn against God. The mourning period, then, is a very crucial time in the relationship between the bereaved and God. It is the time of the true testing of one's faith in God. Because it is a moment of truth between people and God, because it is a time when one may find justification for questions to, complaints about, and rejection of God, it becomes the more urgent, necessary, and crucial that one should, at that very moment, proclaim faith in God and overcome the impulse to reject Him. That is why at the very moment of the burial ceremony, the survivors tear their outer garment (another of the mourning rituals) while reciting the blessing "Blessed art Thou, O Lord our God, who art a righteous judge,"[6] thus accepting God's decree without question or hesitation. A similar, though not identical, practice, was the one that required, in the past

---

5. Job 3; though Job does not explicitly use the expression "Why?" nevertheless that is, at the very least, the gist of his cri de coeur.

6. The blessing is today recited variously at the beginning of the funeral service, when the body is taken to the cemetery, or at the graveside at the conclusion of the prayers. See the *Kol Bo* 71; section 4 of the *Eishel Avraham* on chap. 224 of the *Shulchan Aruch, Orach Chayim, Otzar Halacha,* op. cit. See also the prayer *tziduk hadin* – the justification of the decree – *Yoreh Dei'ah* 401:6, and more on *dayan ha'emet* in *Talmud Bavli, Semachot,* end of chap. 14, and *Berachot* 46b and 54a.

when Jewish courts exercised full judicial authority, even in capital cases, the relatives of a man who was executed to come before the tribunal and extended greetings to the panel as a sign that they, the surviving relatives, harbored no ill feelings toward the judges and that they accepted the verdict as an act of true justice and not personal malice.[7] The same is also true of our relationship with God on the occasion when death strikes. It is necessary at that point for us to affirm our faith in God. The more there is reason to question God, the more one has to proclaim faith in God both in private and in public.

There is no greater test of faith in God than on the occasion of the death of a dear one. We are provoked by the death of loved ones more than by anything else. Death is an outrage. It destroys our love, our hopes, our dreams, our very reason for existing. It tested the patience of Job to its limit. It tests, ever since, the patience and faith of all who experience suffering and death to the limits of their very humanity. That is why at such moments it is important to proclaim faith in God. Only when faith in God is tested most does one's proclamation of it take on true and enduring meaning and purpose. That is why the faith of martyrs means so much. That is why God is extolled by the Mourner's Prayer. It comes from the depths of one's soul and is uttered with a heart full of pain, lips that quiver, eyes that cry, and often an entire body that is broken. Where else and under what other circumstance can one proclaim more sincerely, more fervently, and more meaningfully a faith in God, the Giver of life, than when one mourns – standing in the presence of death at the burial of a loved one and observing the Seven Days of Mourning by identifying oneself with the dead? Nowhere else and under no other circumstance! That is why God is extolled, sanctified, and praised by such a prayer. That is why in reciting that prayer mourners not only proclaim faith in God,[8] in spite of death, but also regain their own life. The recitation of the Mourner's Prayer is a proclamation, also, of one's own triumph over death and a declaration of one's grasp of life. In the Bible, God says to the Children of Israel, "Behold, I have placed before you today life and

7. *Sanhedrin* 46a (Vilna: The Widow and Brothers Romm, 1920): ". . . the relatives come and inquire of the peace of the judges and the peace of the witnesses (*klomar*)) as though they were saying, 'We hold no grudge against you in our hearts, because you rendered true justice.' "

8. Hagaon Rabbi Yechiel Michel Tuchachinsky, *Sefer Gesher Hachayim,* part 3, 2nd ed. (Jerusalem: Nissan Aaron Tuchachinsky, 1960), p. 314.

good, and death and evil . . . and you shall choose life."[9] At the time of loss of a dearly beloved one, we are standing before the choice between life and death, good and evil. When we recite the Mourner's Prayer – the song of hope and life par excellence – we choose life.

May all who mourn, though grievously struck down, have the strength, courage, and wisdom to rise and choose life!

9. Deuteronomy 30:15–19.

56

The Comforting of
Rabbi Yochanan ben Zakkai

One who is drowning will grasp at any straw, we are told by folk wisdom. When one is bereaved, one will welcome any source of comfort. By the same token, people who wish to comfort bereaved relatives or friends may find themselves helpless to do so. In the presence of the bereaved, the comforters are frustrated. They often react by talking loudly, joking, keeping silent, or making innocuous statements. One of the most commonly heard remarks in a house of mourning is, "You are not alone. Such and such went through the same." Or, "I know how you feel. I saw it happen to my dearest relative." All of these comments mean one thing: "Stop complaining. You are not the only one." If people really stopped to consider the meaning of what they say, they might keep silent.

Yet we are told that when one's trouble is shared by others, that in itself is comforting.[1] That may be true, but it does not take the pain and sorrow away from the mourner. Knowing that someone else experienced grief and loss does not remove the mourner's own loss or pain. It may even exacerbate his or her sorrow and disappointment with life.

This, however, is not the only way in which people try to comfort the bereaved. They may also recommend involvement in life,

---

1. *Tzarat rabim chatzi nechamah*, a popular saying. See Even Kaspi on Lamentations 2:13.

getting busy, being philosophical, accepting the inevitable – that every body dies, concentrating on the future, being positive, and then expecting things will be all right. However, for the mourner, nothing is all right. The death of a dear one hurts! It suffocates! It makes you cry! It makes you feel so small and the world around you so big! It makes you cringe into nothing! That is partly what mourning is. For the mourner there must be better answers.

When the son of Rabbi Yochanan ben Zakkai died, we are told, his disciples came to comfort the rabbi.[2] One after another, they came, asked his permission to speak, told him a story from the Bible, and said he should be comforted. Rabbi Yochanan ben Zakkai, however, refused to be comforted. Indeed, he indicated that instead of having comforted him, they had added to his pain and sorrow. Imagine how they must have felt after being told that their words, which were intended to comfort, had brought sorrow and added to the pain of the bereaved instead.

Examining the conversations between Rabbi Yochanan ben Zakkai and his friends, we see that each one had approached him from a different point of view and with a different solution to his bereavement, as though mourning is a disease that varies with each person, which it may well do, and can be cured by a specific medical prescription.

Rabbi Eliezer, his disciple, after gaining permission to speak, drew Rabbi Yochanan ben Zakkai's attention to the fact that Adam, the first man, also had a son who died, yet Adam allowed himself to be comforted, for it is written, "And Adam knew his wife again."[3] We thus see that Adam returned to the normalcy of life and therefore must have been comforted.

Indeed, many a husband finds the love and understanding of his wife, as does a wife that of her husband, most comforting at a time of trouble and suffering. We are told in the Bible that Isaac was comforted after mourning the death of his mother, Sarah, only after he entered the tent of his wife, Rebecca.[4] There is great merit in what Rabbi Eliezer said to his beloved master. In a roundabout way, he simply suggested to him that he should involve himself in the stream of life. Nothing is more symbolic of life than the act of conjugal relations between husband and

---

2. *Avot Derabbi Natan* 14:6.
3. Genesis 4:25.
4. Genesis 24:67.

wife, which is the quintessence of continuity, creativity, partnership with God in giving life, and the very act of defying death itself. (That may be the underlying philosophical reason why conjugal relations are prohibited by Jewish law during the mourning period.[5]) So, therefore, Rabbi Eliezer's advice to his master was to choose life and in that pursuit, to find comfort and consolation at the death of his son. This, however, was not enough for Rabbi Yochanan ben Zakkai.

Rabbi Yochanan ben Zakkai could only reply to this rhetorically, "Is not my own grief big enough for me to bear that you have to add to it Adam's grief?"[6] Knowing of the loss of Adam, Rabbi Yochanan ben Zakkai could feel only the pain and sorrow of Adam as a father who like himself was grieving at the loss of a son. He could not identify himself with Adam's taking comfort, because he could not accept his own return to the world. The death of his son weighed him down. That, alas, is true of so many parents.

I once knew a man who was in mourning for over thirty years at the loss of his son. Until his dying day, he did not have one moment of peace. No matter what his wife, daughter, family, or friends did for him or said to him, he refused to listen. Nay, he could not get over the death of his son, who had died at an early age. Some people are like that. Their own affliction overburdens them. When they see someone else suffer, they take that suffering upon themselves also. Such, too, was the nature of Rabbi Yochanan ben Zakkai. Instead of seeing Adam comforted, he saw him only grieving and took Adam's grief upon himself also. Rabbi Eliezer meant well. His master's pain, alas, was too great to let him come back to life.

When that approach failed to comfort Rabbi Yochanan ben Zakkai, another disciple came to comfort him. Rabbi Yehoshua also requested permission to speak and after receiving it, tried to comfort his master by drawing his attention to the loss of Job. Job, he told him, had sons and daughters, who all died in one day. And yet, in spite of this great tragedy, Job was comforted because, we are told, Job said, "The Lord gave, and the Lord has taken away; blessed be the name of the Lord."[7] Thus, we see that in spite of his great loss and his pain, Job

---

5. *Shulchan Aruch, Yoreh Dei'ah, Hilchot Aveilut* 380:1.

6. *Avot Derabbi Natan* 14:6.

7. Job 1:21 and 2:10. See *Megillah* 25a, "A man is duty bound to bless God over the bad things that happen (to him) as well as the good ones." For the bad things, one says "Blessed be the true Judge—*baruch dayan ha'emet*." See also *Berachot* 54a and Ramban, *Mishneh Torah, Hilchot Berachot* 10:3.

reconciled himself to reality and was comforted. A feeling of resignation and inevitability emerges from the words of Job. The Lord gave. The Lord took. Blessed be the Lord. There is birth. There is death. God is the cause of both.[8] This is God's will. There is none else. That is life! That is what Job tells us. Rabbi Yochanan ben Zakkai did not find such an outlook on life too comforting. Why should his son have died? Had he been born only to die? Are these not the questions every father who loses a son asks? Job found comfort in accepting God's will.

Rabbi Yochanan ben Zakkai could not see how the death of his son could enhance or benefit God's will. He therefore replied to his disciple Rabbi Yehoshua the same way he had replied to Rabbi Eliezer, "Is not my own grief big enough for me to bear that you have to add to it Job's grief?"[9] Rabbi Yochanan ben Zakkai was so overwhelmed with his own state of mourning that he could see only mourning in everybody else as well. Job's comfort was beyond him. Indeed, when we are in grief, we become oblivious to all other things and the world outside us. Grief is all-consuming. It shuts the mourner in and shuts the world out. In its presence there is nothing else. That is why Rabbi Yochanan ben Zakkai could not be comforted by accepting reality as it is, as Job did. His disciple Rabbi Yehoshua meant well. He addressed his master as a philosopher, but Rabbi Yochanan ben Zakkai was just a grieving father. As such, be could feel only pain. He could identify with Job's pain, but not with Job's having been comforted.

Seeing that Rabbi Yochanan ben Zakkai persisted in mourning his son, a third one of his disciples came to comfort him. This one was Rabbi Yosi. He, too, asked permission to speak and having been granted it, proceeded to comfort his master. Rabbi Yosi tried to tell his master that he should listen to the arguments of his disciples and accept their words of comfort. After all, if people say it, he seemed to imply, they must be right. It is, therefore, unfair to ignore the logic, pleading, and example of others. One must follow the path of human nature and conduct. Rabbi Yosi based his reasoning on the story of Aaron the High Priest. According to the Book of Leviticus, Aaron's eldest two sons died suddenly at the same time.[10] When the people expressed their sympathy to him, we are told, "Aaron was silent."[11] That shows that he

---

8. Compare Lamentations 3:36–37.
9. *Avot Derabbi Natan*, op. cit.
10. Leviticus 10:1–2.
11. Ibid., 10:3.

accepted the condolences and was comforted, because that is what it means, to be "silent." Therefore, Rabbi Yosi reasoned, Rabbi Yochanan ben Zakkai should also be comforted. However, Rabbi Yochanan ben Zakkai refused to be comforted by this. He found little comfort in the trouble of others. Instead, he replied to his disciple, "Is not my own grief big enough for me to bear that you have to add to it Aaron's grief?"[12]

Rabbi Yochanan ben Zakkai saw no comfort for himself in the tragedies that other people had suffered, nor did he find comfort in silence. He could not subdue his feelings in quiet acceptance of reality and suspend all judgment of right and wrong in the face of the innocence and suffering he must have perceived in the death of his young son, as Aaron had before him. If anything, the occasion provoked more questioning and bewilderment. The reference to Aaron's loss and the tragic death of his two sons could only increase, not diminish, his own suffering. There are those people who in the face of death find comfort in silence. They withdraw from life and suspend all questions. They accept the mystery of life. Death and birth are both equally great mysteries of life. In the face of the challenge of the mystery of death, Aaron found comfort in silence. Rabbi Yochanan ben Zakkai could not. His sense of human inquisitiveness and his sense of righteousness demanded more. He wanted to know more. He searched for the answer to his painful question, Why? In the absence of an answer, he continued to grieve and mourn.

As Rabbi Yochanan ben Zakkai continued in his bereavement over the death of his son, Rabbi Shimon, yet another of his disciples, came to console him. Asking and receiving Rabbi Yochanan ben Zakkai's permission to speak, he tried to tell him to look to the future, involve himself in the affairs of daily life, and find comfort, maybe, even in having other children. Rabbi Shimon drew on the story of King David in order to press his point of comfort upon his master. He reminded him that King David had a son who died in his childhood and that the king allowed himself to be comforted.[13] Indeed, we know this because it is written in the Bible, "David comforted Bathsheba, his wife, and lived with her, and she gave birth to a son and called his name Solomon."[14]

Therefore, Rabbi Shimon asked his master, should he not learn

---

12. *Avot Derabbi Natan,* op. cit.
13. II Samuel 12:14–23.
14. II Samuel 14:24.

from King David's behavior and also allow himself to be comforted? Rabbi Yochanan ben Zakkai, however, could not accept this argument. Once more he replied, "Is my own grief not big enough for me to bear that you have to add to it David's grief?"[15]

Rabbi Yochanan ben Zakkai could find very little comfort in the way David had adjusted to life by concentrating on the future and letting the past be. Being a man of state and of a practical mind, David could push the sorrow of the present out of his mind by focusing his attention on the future, for the planning and implementation of affairs of state do not allow room for questions about sadness and grief. David had to have a Solomon to whom to entrust the future of his kingdom. When Solomon was born, David found comfort in him because he knew that his own task had been completed. His state would be secure. Rabbi Yochanan ben Zakkai, however, looked at life from a different point of view. He saw the futility of birth. And the death of his son raised the question in his mind of the meaning and purpose of life altogether. Why bother bringing children into the world if we cannot keep them alive? Why give birth if we cannot continue to live? Why participate with God in the great miracle of creating life if we cannot sustain it? Does not the bringing of a new life impose upon us the responsibility for loving, protecting, saving, and keeping it alive? If we cannot do that, then maybe we have no right to give life to others altogether. These are the questions that troubled Rabbi Yochanan ben Zakkai. He could not therefore find comfort in the example of David.

Rabbi Yochanan ben Zakkai was not the first who refused to be comforted. We read in the Bible, for example, that Jacob "refused to be comforted" by his children and family when Joseph was taken from him.[16] The prophet Jeremiah tells us that Rachel, even though long in her grave, was "weeping for her children; she refuses to be comforted for her children because they are not."[17] According to the interpreters, Rachel wept because she saw that all her children had been exiled, none remaining in their own country, and even though they were alive, she refused to be comforted because of her fear about what might yet befall them in exile and because the land was left desolate.[18] How much

---

15. *Avot Derabbi Natan*, op. cit.
16. Genesis 37:34–35.
17. Jeremiah 31:14.
18. David Kimchi (Radak), ibid., and Malbim, ibid.

more cause must a father and mother have to weep and refuse to be comforted than when their child dies?

It seems as though it is natural for us in time of trouble to recoil from bringing children into the world.

In our own time, during the great fear of nuclear war between communist Russia and the West, people debated whether or not to have children. Many postponed doing so for fear that children would only be killed. Through the Bible we are told, according to rabbinic teaching, that Joseph had no children during the great seven-year famine.[19] The *Midrash* relates that Amram, father of Moses, also contemplated not having children, because he was afraid that Pharaoh would kill them.[20] The Talmud tells us further that after the destruction of the Temple, the Jewish people also argued on behalf of not having children. What good is there in bringing them into the world if they are going to be killed?[21] Such arguments based on the despair

---

19. Genesis 41:50. See Rashi. This verse forms the basis for the law of abstinence during times of war and economic upheaval. *Ta'anit* 11a states, "It is prohibited to have marital relations during times of famine, because it says, 'Joseph had two sons before the coming of the years of famine' – *beterem yavo shenat hara'av.*" *Tosefot*, ibid., makes this rule optional. The *gemara* says it does not apply to childless couples – *chasuchei banim*.

20. *Sotah* 12a and *Midrash Rabbah* on *Shemot* 1:13.

21. *Baba Batra* 60b states:

Our rabbis have taught: When the Temple was destroyed for the second time, many Jews became ascetics in order not to eat meat and not to drink wine. Rabbi Yehoshua discussed this with the ascetics and asked them, "My sons, why don't you eat meat and drink wine?" They replied, "How can we eat meat when it used to be offered on the altar (of the Temple) and now it is abolished? How can we drink wine when it used to be offered as a libation on the altar and now it is abolished?" He said to them, "If so, should we not eat bread either, because the meal offerings have been abolished?" "We shall make do with fruit," they answered. "We should not eat fruit either, because the offering of the first fruit has been abolished," he said to them. "We shall make do with the other kinds of fruit," they said. "If so, we should not drink water, because the ceremony of pouring of the water has also been abolished." At that they kept quiet. He said to them, "My sons, come and I will tell you (what to do). Not to mourn at all is impossible, for it has already been decreed. To mourn excessively is (also) impossible, because one does not issue decrees upon the public unless the majority of the people are capable of keeping them."

Therefore this is what the sages have decreed: When one plasters his house he should leave a small part of it unfinished; when a man makes a special meal he should leave one course out; when a woman puts on her ornaments she should leave some off.

Said Rabbi Yishmael ben Elisha: since the day that the Temple was destroyed we should by right have decreed upon ourselves not to eat meat and not to drink wine, but we

brought on by anguish and tragedy are real, but as Miriam said to her father,[22] and the rabbis argued with the survivors, to abstain from procreating only gives victory to death and destruction.[23] If Amram had abstained, Moses would not have been born; if the Jewish people had abstained after the destruction of the Temple, Judaism and Western culture would never have become what they are. The answer to grief is not withdrawal from life but continuity of life. That in a sense is what Rabbi Shimon was hinting at when he told his master about King David's having Solomon and thus showing that he was comforted.

Rabbi Yochanan ben Zakkai, however, was still overcome by his personal grief. The loss of his son must have been devastating for him. He could not think about the world outside when his world inside had collapsed. He could not stop grieving. And he was not the only one who could not stop. "In the day of my trouble," King David tells us, "I seek the Lord; with my hands uplifted, [my eye] streams with tears in the night without ceasing: my soul refuses to be comforted."[24] David refused to be comforted because his troubles persisted. He saw no way out of them. As long as he was in trouble, he could not, and therefore he refused to be comforted. When a parent feels the pain of the loss of a son, he becomes enwrapped in it. He is constantly in pain and sorrow. Therefore, he cannot be comforted. Rabbi Yochanan ben Zakkai constantly felt the pain of the death of his son. He, too, therefore could not be comforted.

---

do not proclaim any decree unless the majority of the public can adhere to it. Now since the wicked government that decreed bad and harsh decrees upon us prohibiting us to keep the Torah and the *mitzvot* and forbidding us to practice circumcision, which some say brings salvation to our sons, has come to power, it is only right that we should decree upon ourselves not to marry, not to have children,* but [by doing this], we would bring about the destruction of the descendants of Abraham by our own actions. Therefore, it is the best to leave the Jews to themselves. Let them better do things [which by right should be forbidden] out of ignorance** than out of spite.

Tosafot says it applies only to those who already have two children, a boy and a girl.

**Rabbeinu Gershom and the *Tosafot* comment on this: Who can tell if they [Jews] would abide by such a decree. Therefore, they might not live up to it and marry anyway and thus transgress upon the decree of the rabbis and commit a sin. Rashi states on the same: They might marry out of ignorance because they would think there is no prohibition against marriage.

22. See n. 20, op. cit.

23. *Baba Batra*, op. cit.

24. Psalms 77:3.

Must we conclude that only those who are less enveloped in the pain of the loss of their dear ones can be comforted, and not the others? What is the end of the story of Rabbi Yochanan ben Zakkai's mourning?

We are told that, finally, Rabbi Yochanan ben Zakkai's great disciple Rabbi Eleazar ben Aroch came to pay his condolences and to comfort his master. Something happened, however, when he came, that made the fact of his very presence different. When Rabbi Yochanan ben Zakkai saw Rabbi Eleazar coming, he said to his attendant, "Quickly, take my clothes and follow me to the bathhouse. This man is a distinguished personality, and I cannot appear before him as I am."[25] Rabbi Yochanan ben Zakkai had an inner urge of respect for his disciple, which prompted him to take off his mourning garments and dress himself properly in order to greet Rabbi Eleazar ben Aroch.

When Rabbi Eleazar ben Aroch came in, he sat down, as is the custom in a house of mourning,[26] and began to speak. He told Rabbi Yochanan ben Zakkai a parable. Said he to him. "This situation is compared to the following story. There was a man with whom a king deposited an article of great value. Each day the man wept and shouted, 'Woe is me! When will I be free of the responsibility of this trust in peace?' You, too, my master, had a son versed in the Torah, who had studied the Five Books of Moses, the Books of the Prophets, the Holy Writings, *Mishnah, halachah* [law], and *Agudat* [homiletics]. Without any sin he has departed from this world. Surely you should derive comfort from having returned your trust intact! Therefore, you have to be comforted because you have returned that which was entrusted to you in peace."[27]

---

25. *Avot Derabbi Natan,* op. cit.

26. Job 2:12–13–*Shulchan Aruch, Yoreh Dei'ah* 387:1; Rambam, *Mishneh Torah, Hilchot Eivel* 13:3. The *lechem mishneh* says that the *Rambam* bases on the *Alfasi* his statement that those who come to console the bereaved must sit on the ground. But in our version of the *gemara,* we do not have this text.

Rashi, however, in *Moed Katan* 24b, says, *"ein meva'arin ela al mitah zekufah*–Those who come to provide the bereaved with the meal of consolation do so only on an erect bench." Says Rashi, "The people who are doing the consoling are sitting down." The *Nimukei Yosef* on Ran (Rabbi Nisim), in *Moed Katan* 18a, states that the custom for those who come to console the bereaved is based on Job: Those who come to console are not allowed to sit down except on the ground just like the bereaved ones are sitting, because, it says, "And they sat with him" (Job 2: that is, "as he did–*kemotoh*").

27. *Avot Derabbi Natan,* op. cit.

When he finished, Rabbi Yochanan ben Zakkai said to him, "Eleazar my son, you have comforted me as men can comfort."[28] Rabbi Eleazar comforted his master as much as it is in the power of people to do so.

What is it that Rabbi Eleazar said that comforted Rabbi Yochanan ben Zakkai, and why are we told that Rabbi Yochanan ben Zakkai dressed up in order to receive his disciple? We learn several things both from the encounter between master and student and from what Rabbi Eleazar said.

1. The fact that Rabbi Yochanan ben Zakkai removed his mourning clothes, bathed, and dressed up before he received Rabbi Eleazar is highly symbolic and significant. The removal of the mourning clothes showed that he was already prepared to come out of his state of mourning and that his grief was subsiding. His dressing up indicates that he was ready to step back into the world of activity and normality from which he had withdrawn when he was in mourning. We see in his outward behavior that a radical inner change was taking place, the most important one being that of showing a readiness to move, to act, to change, and to come back to society. When his other disciples came and spoke to him, he displayed toward all of them a passive, uninterested, and detached personality. When Rabbi Eleazar came, he suddenly became active, he moved, and he did things.

It is hard to say what brought on this sudden change. Perhaps it was the passage of time. Perhaps it was the sudden appearance of Rabbi Eleazar. Perhaps it was a combination of both. It remains that we now see a changed Rabbi Yochanan ben Zakkai. We see a man who is alive and active again. We see a master who is conscious of his appearance in the presence of his disciple and aware of his social responsibilities. We must therefore conclude that Rabbi Yochanan ben Zakkai underwent an attitude change. Whereas before the appearance of Rabbi Eleazar his attitude had been one of withdrawal, after the appearance of Rabbi Eleazar his attitude was that of positive involvement. He now was displaying by his behavior that he had the right attitude toward grief and comfort. Even though he still grieved, he already was showing that he would be comforted. He had a positive attitude.

In stoic philosophy, we are taught that we have no control over life and events, except over one thing. We can control our

---

28. Ibid.

attitude.[29]How we look at the world is up to us. As the rabbis say, "Everything is in the hands of heaven, except the fear of heaven."[30] We have control only over our attitude toward life and toward the events that confront us. If we were to only develop the right attitude, we would be able to cope with all things in life. Without the right attitude we can cope with nothing.

This is also true of grief and comfort. One must first want to be comforted before one will be comforted. One must show a positive attitude. One must have willpower and be open to the outside world before one can enter it. There is no use comforting or counseling anyone if that one does not want to be comforted. Rabbi Yochanan ben Zakkai threw off his mourning clothes and dressed up to show us symbolically that he was ready for comfort. His attitude toward life had changed. The appearance of Rabbi Eleazar had jolted him back to life, bringing out in him his positive attitude toward comfort. It was the beginning of the process of healing!

2. Rabbi Eleazar did not speak to his master about other people. Unlike his colleagues, who had tried to tell their master to imitate others and learn from their actions, Rabbi Eleazar appealed to his master directly. He told him a parable with which he could identify. In one and the same story he accomplished two things. He praised his

---

29. Epictetus, *Discourses*, Book I, Great Books of the Western World, vol. 12, trans. George Long (Chicago: Encyclopedia Britannica, 1952), pp. 129–131: ". . . All things are from God." Marcus Aurelius, *Meditations*, Great Books, ibid., p. 263:

> For the whole earth is a point, and how small a nook in it is this thy dwelling, and how few are there in it, and what kind of people are they who will praise thee. This then remains: Remember to retire into this little territory of thy own, and above all do not distract or strain thyself, but be free, and look at things as a man, as a human being, as a citizen, as a mortal. But among the things readiest to thy hand be these, which are two. One is that things do not touch the soul, for they are external and remain immovable, but *our perturbations come only from the opinion which is within.* The other is that all these things, which thou seest, change immediately and will no longer be; and constantly bear in mind how many of these changes thou hast witnessed. *The universe is transformation; life is opinion.*

30. *Berachot* 33b.

Rashi makes the following observation on the above: Everything which befalls man is by the hand of God, for example whether one is tall or short, poor or rich, wise or foolish, light or dark, everything is in the hands of God, but whether one is a righteous or a wicked man does not depend on heaven. This (God) handed over into the hands of man and He gave him two paths (upon which to go). Man should choose the path of the fear of heaven.

See also Rambam, *Mishneh Torah, Hilchot Teshuvah* 5:1, and *Tosafot* on *Megillah* 25a for a discussion of this topic. *Tosefot* concurs with Rashi.

son, which, naturally, gladdened the father's heart, and he praised the father, Rabbi Yochanan ben Zakkai himself. This was the effect of his telling him how good and pious his son had been and how well he had discharged his duties as a father. Rabbi Yochanan ben Zakkai could relate to the man in the parable, who was charged with the responsibility of guarding the king's property. Like that man, Rabbi Yochanan ben Zakkai, too, had been entrusted with a son, a human being, the creation of the kings. God gave him his son, so that he should be his father and he should guard him, rear him, and set him on the right path in life. These are the duties of a father. A father is only a guardian. All children, like all human beings, must return to their Creator.

Rabbi Yochanan ben Zakkai could identify with this story. It appealed to him directly. He did not have to compare himself to Adam, Job, Aaron, or David. They had their own burdens and grief and he had his own. However, he could relate to the man in the story. It had meaning. It was relevant. The man was he. The valuable object was his son. Therefore he found comfort in it.

3. Rabbi Yochanan ben Zakkai must have found Rabbi Eleazar most comforting when he told him that he returned his son in peace, as did the man who returned the object to his king. How reassuring it must be to know that one has discharged one's duties fully. That indeed is the meaning of Rabbi Eleazar's message to his master, when he assures him that his son was a good young man and that he, his father, has fulfilled his duties toward him. He, in other words, has done his work well for God, Who had entrusted him with the task of caring for his son's life. To know that is to know freedom. It is to be free of guilt, for the greatest burden that survivors often carry is the one of feeling guilty at the death of their loved one.

Psychologists—Freud foremost among them—have pointed out that survivors have an enormous feeling of guilt when a loved one dies.[31] This is a deeply rooted human feeling, traceable to the begin-

---

31. Sigmund Freud, *Civilization and Its Discontents,* Great Books, vol. 54, pp. 792–96, and Sigmund Freud, *New Introductory Lectures on Psychoanalysis* (New York: W. W. Norton, 1933) pp. 149–50:

As to the origin of this unconscious need for punishment there can be, I think, no doubt. It behaves like a part of the conscience, like the prolongation of conscience into the unconscious, and it must have the same origin as conscience; that is to say, it will correspond to a piece of aggressiveness which has been internalized and taken over by the superego. If only the words were less incongruous, we should be justified, for all practical

ning of time. Through studies that have been made, it has been shown in recent times to exist among the survivors of the Holocaust,[32] of

---

purposes, in calling it an *unconscious sense of guilt*. People in whom this unconscious sense of guilt is dominant distinguish themselves under analytic treatment by exhibiting what is so unwelcome from the point of view of prognosis—a negative therapeutic reaction. In the normal course of events, if one gives a patient the solution of a symptom, at least the temporary disappearance of that symptom should result; with these patients, on the contrary, the effect is a momentary intensification of the symptom and the suffering that accompanies it. It often needs only a word of praise of their behavior during the cure, the utterance of a few words of hope as to the progress of the analysis, to bring about an unmistakable aggravation of their condition. A nonanalyst would say that *they were lacking in the will to recovery;* from the analytical point of view their behavior will appear as an expression of an unconscious *sense of guilt which favors illness with its attendant suffering and handicaps.*

Robert Jay Lifton, *History and Human Survival* (New York: Random House, 1970), p. 169. In discussing the feelings of the survivors of Hiroshima, he says:

A central conflict of this *hibakusha* [defined on page 118 as "survivor" (or survivors)], but which literally means "explosion-affected person" [or persons] identity is the problem of what I have come to speak of as a *survival priority*—the inner question of why one has survived while so many have died, the inevitable self-condemnation in the face of others' death. *For the survivor can never, inwardly, simply conclude that it was logical and right for him, and not others, to survive. Rather, I would hold, he is bound by an unconscious perception of organic social balance, which makes him feel that his survival was made possible by others' death: if they had not died, he would have to; and if he had not survived, someone else would have* [author's italics]. This kind of guilt as it relates to survival priority may well be that most fundamental to human existence. Also contributing to the survivors' sense of guilt are feelings (however dimly recalled) of relief, even joy, that it was the other and not he who died. And his guilt may be accentuated by previous death wishes toward parents who had denied him nurturance he craved or toward siblings who competed for this nurturance, whether this guilt is directly experienced in relationship to the actual death of those family members or indirectly, through unconsciously relating such wishes to the death of any "other," however anonymous.

32. Lifton, ibid., p. 171. The author cites William G. Niederland's study, "Problems of the Survivor: Part I: Some Remarks on the Psychiatric Evolution of Emotional Disorders in Survivors of Nazi Persecution," *Journal of the Hillside Hospital* 10 (1961): 233–247.

. . . whose "psychological imprint" in concentration camp survivors . . . includes elements of depressive mood, withdrawal, apathy, outbursts of anger, and self-deprecatory attitudes which, in extreme cases, lead to a "living corpse" appearance; this is in turn attributed to their owing their survival to maintaining an existence of a "walking corpse" while their fellow inmates succumbed . . . in the Nazi concentration camps, in addition to the more prolonged physical and psychological assault upon identity and character structure, the problem of survival priority was . . . directly experienced: Each inmate became aware that either he or someone else would be chosen for death, and went to great length to maintain his own life at the expense of the known or anonymous "other."

Hiroshima and Nagasaki,[33] and of other tragedies.[34] Why do survivors

---

Anna Pawelczynska, *Values and Violence in Auschwitz–a Sociological Analysis*, trans. Catherine S. Leach (Los Angeles: University of California Press, 1979), p. 139. The author introduces a new and very interesting observation about an additional aspect of life among the survivors, which contributed to their feeling of guilt. She says:

> A person who made no revision or reductions in the hierarchy of moral standards previously acknowledged had to perish if he applied them in an absolute way. Such a prisoner could only survive if he benefitted from the help and care of those who infringed some of those standards or eliminated them from their system of values. *A prisoner who in his mind remained faithful to his previous system of values, but in his daily living arrangements had to break them lived with a destructive feeling of guilt,* and either perished or reduced his standards in such a way as to lessen the dissonance between convictions and his conduct.
>
> The pattern of diminishment was similar no matter whether the process of reducing moral standards occurred on the existential or the intellectual plane and regardless of the religious or ideological values which had shaped a particular person. This pattern took the course of (1) reduction of various systems of morality to one system that countenanced those values universally recognized as the most important, (2) reinterpretation of norms so that a diminishment of their content and/or scope took place, and (3) elimination of norms that were dysfunctional in camp condition.

33. Robert Jay Lifton, *Death in Life–Survivors of Hiroshima* (New York: Random House, 1969), pp. 40–43ff. The author cites cases of survivors who feel guilty because their relatives or friends died and who express remorse for not having done more to help them.

> . . . "If I had been a little older or stronger I could have rescued her . . . Even now I still hear my mother's voice calling me to help her . . ."
>
> "I feel sorry for him . . . His dying . . . still gives me very deep emotions . . . he . . . went so many places . . . to look for me and because he preceded me in death . . ." [p. 40].
>
> "I regret when I think back on it . . . Why didn't I go to see my father when he was dying? . . ." [p. 41].

Lifton also makes the following observations:

> In all of these instances guilt is magnified by previous events felt toward family members– and the survivor can never be inwardly certain to what degree his "neglect" of a parent, child, or spouse is related to such prior feelings . . . [p. 41].
>
> Here ignorance, conflicting responsibilities, psychic closing off, and ambivalence are inextricably intertwined in their contribution to guilt. Guilt toward family members could also be expressed more directly [p. 41].
>
> One man told me . . . of his inability to rescue a nephew killed in the room next to him . . . he inwardly wondered how great an effort he had made. I also heard many stories of children and parents separated from one another . . . in which I could detect unconscious rhythms . . . of guilt-anger-abandonment alternating with those of relief, gratitude, restored nurturance, with the guilt reasserting itself particularly strongly where one of the people involved eventually died [p. 42].
>
> Sometimes survivors could not help each other because of their additional personal problems and they said that ". . . Even stronger than thoughts about life and death was this feeling of loneliness and fear . . . of having no home and no family . . ." (p. 43).
>
> ". . . feelings of abandonment, helplessness, and death anxiety greatly interfered with her capacity for providing maternal care . . . [p. 40].

feel guilty? The answer may never be known. Suffice it to say they feel guilty because they feel they may have wished death on their loved ones, that their loved one took their place, that they did not do enough to save their loved one, or that they may have offended him or her during their loved one's lifetime, never made up, or did not do enough in general. Whatever the cause of our feeling of guilt may be, it is expressed in grief and mourning. Sometimes it is shown in excessive mourning, and the more we mourn, the more we may feel we had not love enough for, or owed it to, the departed. The more mourning, the more guilt. It is therefore logical that the more a person feels responsible for the lot in life of others, let alone for one's own family, the more one will feel guilty for not having saved them from suffering, death, and destruction and the more one will mourn their loss. Indeed, there is no greater cause of guilt than the death of a beloved child for whom parents naturally feel such a great responsibility and the natural urge to do all in their power to keep the child alive. When parents lose a child, they feel not only the natural pain of loss, separation, and grief but also the devastating blow of inadequacy, failure, and a guilty conscience, because they may believe that somewhere, somehow, they did something wrong or did not do enough to save their child. Such a feeling of guilt can be devastating.

Therefore, no greater good can be done for us than to remove such guilt. When we can be shown that we are not guilty for our own shortcomings; that we are not responsible for our misdeeds; that we may continue a normal life as long as we own up to the real nature of our own self and do not expect of ourselves God-like acts that determine the life and death of others, of thinking of ourselves as being perfect, or of expecting to be able to do the superhuman and recognize our own limitations, pay restitution for the harm we may cause others, and acknowledge that there is a higher power than we, then we have no reason to continue to feel guilty. (That may be a reason why Judaism forbids excessive mourning.)[35]

I encountered many analogous patterns of behavior . . . In addition to fainting, these included . . . impairment of mobility, vision, hearing, and speech . . . [p. 45] [as well as] ". . . self-loathing, which contains not only overt shame but also hidden guilt . . . [p. 76]. *We noted in Hiroshima the special intensity of the guilt of parents surviving their children* [p. 489].

34. Lifton, op. cit.

35. *Moed Katan 27b*: Rabbi Yehudah said in the name of Rav, "A person who mourns in extreme over a departed (relative) will soon cry over another person (who

THE COMFORTING OF RABBI YOCHANAN BEN ZAKKAI

One of the great things that Judaism has offered mankind is the concept of forgiveness. The greatest thing that happened to the ancient Israelites, the rabbis teach, was that they entered the Temple in Jerusalem guilty and were able to come out innocent.[36] The removal of guilt was the great gift that God gave them when they built the Temple. "Happy are you, O Israel, who are purified in the presence of your Father in heaven, and happy are you that the Father in heaven

---

will die)." Rambam, *Mishneh Torah, Hilchot Eivel* 13:10: "One should not mourn excessively over the dead, because it says, 'Do not cry over the dead and do not mourn over him'" (Jeremiah 22:10), that is, more than it is usually done, which is the "natural" custom of the world (*minhago shel olam*). He who mourns more than it is the natural custom of the world to do so is a fool. How then should one conduct oneself? The first three days are for crying; the first seven days (including the first three) are for eulogizing; the first thirty days one does not shave (or have a haircut). *Shulchan Aruch, Yoreh Dei'ah, Hilchot Aveilut* 384a gives a detailed breakdown of the laws of mourning during these stages of bereavement. What the Rambam calls *minhago shel olam*. The natural custom of the world the *Nimukei Yosef* (ibid.) calls more than what the sages have decreed (*yoter mimah shetiknu chachamim*).

36. *Berachot* 18a. When Rabbi Sheishet finished praying on a Fast Day, he would say:

> Master of the universe, You know that all the time *when the Temple existed, a man who committed a sin would bring a sacrifice* as an offering *and* even though only its fat and blood would be offered up, yet *atonement would be made for him with that alone*. Now, I have fasted and my fat and blood were diminished, may it be Thy will that my fat and my blood which were diminished (from me) should be regarded (by You) as though I have offered it before You upon the altar. Therefore, please show me your favors. (*Midrash Rabbah, Bamidbar* 18:17; *Berachot* 17a.)

The Israelites said. "*When the Temple existed, we used to offer fat and consecrated parts of the animals and we found atonement.* Now we offer our own fat and blood and souls. May it be Thy will that it shall be an atonement for us" (*Midrash Tehilim* 25:3). "*When the Temple existed, a man who committed a sin would bring a sacrifice and it was an atonement for them.* Now when we do not have sacrifices, let our suffering be considered as a peace offering."

The *Tur Orach Chayim, Hilchot Ta'anit* 565, states that it is good to recite after the conclusion of the supplicatory (*Tachanun*) prayers at the end of the *Minchah* service the following:

> Master of the universe, it is known before You that when the Temple existed, a man who sinned would bring a sacrifice of which only its fat and blood would be sacrificed, and You in your great compassion would accept it as an atonement for him. Now because of our transgressions the Temple was destroyed. We have no Temple and no *Kohen* to atone for us. Therefore, may it be Your will that my fat and my blood which was diminished today be acceptable before You as though it were the fat that was placed upon Your altar and because of that may I find favor with You!

purifies you!"[37] the rabbis proclaim. The greatest contribution of the Temple, therefore, was to restore people to a normal state of existence by removing from them their feeling of guilt for their own shortcomings. We were not made perfect. We are accepted for what we are in the eyes of God.

There was no other man who must have cared as much for his son as did Rabbi Yochanan ben Zakkai, if we are to judge him by the way he cared for the Jewish people. Rabbi Yochanan ben Zakkai lived at the time of the destruction of the second Temple. When Titus destroyed Jerusalem and the Temple, Rabbi Yochanan ben Zakkai, at the risk of his own life, at the hands of both the Zealot defenders of the burning city and the ravaging Roman legionnaires, escaped the besieged city in order to establish a center of Jewish learning elsewhere and thus ensure the survival of Judaism and the Jews.[38] No one else is given as much credit for the survival of Judaism and Jewry after the destruction of the Temple than he.[39] He who cared so much and loved his people so much must have surely loved no less his own flesh and blood, his own

---

37. *Yoma* 85b in the name of Rabbi Akiva. The concept of teshuvah – repentance – is in large measure based on the need to remove guilt feelings. The day of Yom Kippur is set aside for that very same reason – to remove guilt from those who observe it. The thrust of the Yom Kippur prayers is to show, among other things, (1) how frail man is, (2) how compassionate and forgiving God is, and (3) how God forgives man and gives him another chance to start anew, if only he would acknowledge his guilt and atone.

True, guilt is not removed automatically, but it is removed nevertheless, and man can start life free and fresh all over again. That is the theme of Yom Kippur. Here are a few random citations from the Yom Kippur Service (*High Holy Day Prayer Book*, trans. Philip Birnbaum [New York: Hebrew Publishing Co., 1951]).

On this day shall atonement be made for you to cleanse you; from all your sins shall you be clean before the Lord [p. 508].

Thou art the Forgiver of Israel, the Pardoner of the tribes of Yeshurun in every generation . . . Who dost pardon and forgive our iniquities and the iniquities of the people Israel and dost remove our ill deeds year by year [p. 770].

While the breath of life is yet in man, God looks for His creatures to repent.

To grant man life and to prosper him [p. 794].

Thou hast no desire for anyone to die, but that he return from his evil way and live.

38. Rabbi Yochanan ben Zakkai's heroic and farsighted escape from Jerusalem during the Roman siege marked a turning point in Jewish life. Rabbi Yochanan ben Zakkai is credited with the establishment of Yavneh as a center of learning and revival after the Temple was destroyed in 70 C.E. See *Gittin* 56a-b: "*ten li Yavneh vechachameha*" – "Give me *Yavneh* and the sages" – was his only request of the Roman; see n. 39.

39. Shmuel Sarai. *Tekufat Hamishnah Vehatalmud*, in *Toldot Am Yisrael*, vol. 1, *Biymei Kedem*, ed. H. H. Ben-Sasson (Tel Aviv: Devir, 1969), p. 305: "For all practical

son. Surely he who felt so much responsibility for the safety and survival of others, albeit it was his people, must have also felt no less about the life of his own son. One can therefore easily imagine how guilty he must have felt for failing to preserve his son in life. One can imagine how loudly the proverbial words "but my own vineyard I did not watch"[40] must have been ringing in his ears.

Little wonder that he could not stop mourning and grieving over the death of his son. Little wonder that he would not accept the words of comfort that his disciples offered him. He was too deep in guilt because of his personal failure to save his own son!

Rabbi Eleazar, with his parable, addressed this problem. He told his master that he need not blame himself. He had kept his faith with his son and with God. His son had been a righteous person and a scholar. The rabbi had brought him up well. Therefore he had done all he could. Now he had returned him to God, Who had placed him in his trust. There is no need to feel any guilt. When Rabbi Yochanan ben Zakkai heard that, he was comforted.[41]

---

purposes Rabbi Yochanan ben Zakkai starts, whether with or without the knowledge of the (Roman) authorities, to rebuild anew the Jewish life and to bridge over the void which was created by the destruction of the Temple." See also Naftal, Avraham Moshe *Talmud Veyotzrav*, vol. 1. *Dorot Hatana'yim* (Tel Aviv: Yehoshua Orenstein, Yavneh Publishing), p. 21.

   "Rabbi Yochanan ben Zakkai is deservedly (*betzedek* – rightly) regarded as the first among the builders of the nation and its providers after the destruction of the Temple." Also Max L. Margolis and Alexander Marx, *A History of the Jewish People* (Philadelphia: Jewish Publication Society, 1947) pp. 205-207, and especially H. Graetz, *History of the Jews*, vol. 2, (Philadelphia: Jewish Publication Society, 1991) pp. 322-323. After describing the disaster of the Jews following the destruction of the Temple, Graetz continues, "What was to be the future of the Jewish nation, of Judaism?"

   The *Sanhedrin*, which had given laws to the entire community and had regulated its religious life, disappeared with the fall of Jerusalem. Who would step into the breach and render continued existence a possibility?

   There now appeared a man who seemed made to save the essential doctrines of Judaism and restore some amount of strength to the nation, so that it might continue to live and that threatened decay might be averted. This man was Yochanan the son of Zakkai. He labored like the prophets during the first exile in Babylon – but by other means – in order to maintain the life of the Jewish nation: he reanimated its frozen limbs and by infusing fresh energy into its actions, consolidated its dispersed members into one whole.

   40. Song of Songs 1:6.

   41. Rabbi Yochanan obviously was in a deep depression brought on by, among other things, a feeling of guilt, which was discussed and which he was consciously or subconsciously struggling to overcome. The following passage by Professor Lifton will

We can now summarize the message of the comforting of Rabbi Yochanan ben Zakkai.

The disciples who first came to comfort him at the loss of his son tried to draw his attention to the fact that he was not the only one who had ever suffered a loss. Others had also lost their children, but they all were comforted. One did this by returning to family life; another, by saying it was the will of God; a third, by keeping silent; and a fourth, by turning to the future. However, Rabbi Yochanan ben Zakkai found little comfort in this. The pain of others only increased his own pain. The fact that others could find comfort by turning away from their trouble did not remove the suffering he inflicted upon himself by his own guilt. His disciple Rabbi Eleazar pointed out to him that before he could be comforted, he must be ready to accept comfort. He told him to look at himself and not at others for comfort, and, finally, he told him

---

further illuminate this problem. (Robert J. Lifton, *The Broken Connection* [New York: Simon and Schuster, 1979].)

> . . . guilt had great importance to depression . . . Freud connected mourning for dead parents with melancholia . . . [p. 190] . . . most psychiatrists continue to believe that guilt is central to depression . . . [p. 191]. He continues to say that there are two forms of static guilt: One is that of self-condemnation and the other is that of numbed guilt.
>
> Numbed guilt is one of the keys to understanding depression and it plays a major part in all psychic disorders . . . This state of existence leads to . . . a need to behave as if dead [or deadened]; death or killing moreover, is perceived . . . as deserving and necessary and brought on by the self . . . [p. 192]. [And furthermore . . .] the problem of depression is . . . the imbalance of static and animating forms of guilt. Whether self-lacerating or numbed, the guilt in depression is not self-perpetuating. There is a characteristic inability to achieve animating relationships to guilt, to connect self-blame with imagery of change and possibly with imagery beyond guilt. The depressive's struggle against inner death, then, is not so much toward eliminating guilt as toward achieving an animating relationship to it . . .
>
> One could in fact, characterize depression as a disorder of blame. There can be fluctuation between self-blame (guilt) and blaming others (anger) but more important is the tendency of both forms of blaming to the enmeshed in static structures. When systems of blaming are impaired, so is one's overall moral and cause-and-effect cosmology . . . One becomes prone to depression not because of tendencies toward guilt or anger per se, but toward guilt and anger that, because static, cannot do their job in helping one to cope with loss . . . guilt, like anger, either contributes to the deadening process in depression or may vitalize alternatives to depression in coping with loss . . . these alternatives–deadliness versus vitality–are at the heart of the deep ambivalence of the depressed person. The issue is not so much internalized ambivalence toward a lost love object, as Freud thought, as an unresolved inner struggle, around the mind's (and sometimes the body's) dying or living . . . [pp. 192–94].

Reading these lines, we can see the struggle Rabbi Yochanan ben Zakkai was going through. In his case, obviously, the will to live won out.

that he was only a man. He need not feel guilty. He had done all he could in keeping his son alive and making a great human being of him. Everything else was in the hands of God. That means his son's life as well. He was only his son's trustee. The son belonged to God, as all human beings do, and as all creation does. He could be happy that he was able to carry out his trusteeship. Rabbi Yochanan ben Zakkai accepted this argument. He was therefore comforted!

May all who mourn realize the truth of this teaching and find comfort in its message!

57

The Lessons from Bereavement

Bereavement is traumatic. No one who is not in the midst of it can fathom what a person experiences when bereaved. No one should pretend that he can. The best one can do is try to understand and empathize with the bereaved.

The rabbis, in speaking of bereavement, understood it well. They never pretended to feel what the bereaved felt. They tried only to show how much they empathized with them. They always regarded it as a most intimate, profoundly personal, and deeply emotional experience. They used emotive and descriptive words when speaking of it. A man who lost his wife had his days turn dark or his steps shortened or was as though the Temple were destroyed in his lifetime. A parent who lost a child was compared to one who had to return a precious gift. Martyrs had a unique place in heaven. And so on. The Talmud also says that when one has to make arrangements for the dead, one is absolved from performing any of the commandments of the Torah.[1] The usual

---

1. *Shulchan Aruch, Yoreh Dei'ah, Hilchot Aninut* 341: "He (the mourner) is absolved from keeping all the *mitzvot* mentioned in the Torah."

See the *Gilyon Maharsha* for a list of occasions on which one is absolved from performing the *mitzvot*.

The *Pitchei Teshuvah* on the same topic points out that this applies only to the positive commandments and not the negative ones.

For a discussion of the topic of whether *aveilut* and *aninut* are *mide'oraita* or *miderabanan*

reason is that one is too busy with the needs of the dead,[2] and since we

---

(Torah or rabbinic laws), see the *Tur, Yoreh Dei'ah* 398 and the *Bach* and *Beit Yosef* commentaries.

Now, the original source for this law is in *Semachot* 10:1 as follows: "As long as a mourner still has to attend to the needs of the burial of the dead [*shemeito mutal lefanav* does not mean literally that the corpse is lying in the mourner's presence or confines but rather 'as long as one has to deal with the burial arrangements' (see *nachalat Ya'akov*, ibid]), one is absolved from reciting the *Shema* and prayers and keeping any (all) of the *mitzvot* mentioned in the Torah." These very same words are repeated in *Berachot* 17b where *Tosefot* interpolates the word *tefilin* after *tefilah* – prayer – and also in *Moed Katan* 23b (which is the source of *Tosefot's* interpolation of *tefilin*). See also *Berachot* 3:1. (The *Peirush Meba'al Sefer Chareidim* on the above expresses the same opinion as the *Nachalat Ya'akov*, ibid.) See also the Rambam on *Hilchot Aveilut* 4:6. Rashi in *Berachot* 18a states also, "Whenever the mourner has the duty to bury the dead it is stated that *meito mutal lefanav* – the dead is lying before him [in his presence]."

2. Rashi on *Berachot* 17b: The *Peirush Meba'al Sefer Chareidim* on same in *Talmud Yerushalmi, Berachot*, ibid., cites Rabeinu Yonah, who says that even if one wants to recite the *Shema*, one is not allowed to do so even though the recitation of the *Shema* deals with the acceptance of the yoke of the heavenly kingdom (presumably because one cannot give full attention to God in the presence of one's dead and because death – *To'omah* – impurity, and God – *kedushah* – holiness – do not go together). See also the *Hagahot Maimoniyot* on the Rambam, ibid., who says that this law may be due to the principle of *kavod hameit* – respect for the dead.

Rabbi Boon, in *Berachot* 10:1 (*gemara* p. 22a), states that one is absolved from putting on *tefilin*, because it is written therein, "In order that you shall remember the day when you went out of Egypt all the days of your life" (Deuteronomy 16:3). Rabbi Boon quotes this verse because, like the third and fourth passages of the Torah, in Exodus 13:1–10 and 13:11–16, which are included in the *tefilin*, it too deals with the Exodus from Egypt). "[That means] on days on which one deals with the living and not on days on which one deals with the dead." *Tosefot* in *Berachot* 10:1 follows this view.

The *Talmud Yerushalmi* on the same page (ibid.) discusses the reason why one is forbidden to recite the *Shema* even if one wants to do it out of personal piety (*machmir al atzmo*). It gives two reasons: one, because it is disrespectful to the dead (one cannot be pious at the expense of others), and two, because the mourner has no one else to take his place to attend to the dead. (The *halachah* is based on the principle of *kavod hameit*.)

The Rambam, on *Berachot* 4:7, however, holds that whoever wishes to keep the *mitzvot* may do so even if absolved from doing so because of the need to attend to the dead. However, the *Beit Yosef* – *Yoreh Dei'ah*, ibid., and most of the *poskim* do not allow a mourner to keep the *mitzvot* when he is an *onein*. In other words, they do not hold the view that he is *patur* – absolved of doing so – but that he is *asur* – forbidden to do so. That is, when the *gemara* uses the word "*patur*," it means *asur* in this case. For a detailed discussion of the topic, see *Mareh Panim* on *Berachot* 4:7, p. 22a.

A different and beautiful explanation of this law is given by Reish Lakish in *Midrash Rabbah*, Leviticus (*Tzav*) 98. In discussing the question of the Peace Offerings and who

can do only one thing at one time in one place, therefore those who engage in performing one commandment are absolved from the duty of performing any other commandments.[3] However, I would like to suggest that the rabbis teach us that when one has his dead father or mother before him, one is free of all commandments in the Torah because in the state of bereavement, as some suggest, one's mind does not work well,[4] and one is as good as being dead oneself. In short, the bereaved are also in a state of death. The bereaved's life is in a state of "suspension." To mourn is to identify with the dead. How, then, do you comfort and console the dead? How do you lead the quasi-dead back to life? That is the task of comforting and consoling the bereaved!

One way of doing it is to be there, to stretch out an open hand, to

---

may or may not bring a Peace Offering, he says, "Whoever is at peace (*mi shehu shalom*) brings a Peace Offering. *Ve'ein*–therefore, an *onein* does not bring a Peace Offering" (because he has no peace of mind, being in a state of mourning).

The *Etz Yosef*, commenting on this, states "Because an *onein* is not allowed to eat of the sacrifices, since it is written, 'I have not eaten thereof *be'oni*–when I was an *onein*' (Deuteronomy 26:14)."

3. As long as a mourner is engaged in making arrangements for the dead (that is, all the time until the funeral–cases in which the transportation of the body, etc., is taken care of by funeral homes should be dealt with separately), that mourner is engaged in performing a *mitzvah*. When such mourners stop in order to perform another *mitzvah*, for example, to recite the *Shema*, they automatically disrupt their performance of the *mitzvah* of attending to the dead. This is not allowed. One cannot "drop" one *mitzvah* in order to perform another one. (However, to merely answer "amen" is not an interruption, *mareh panim*, ibid.).

In *Sukkah* 26a, Rabbi Yosi Haglili says, "Whoever is engaged in the performance of one *mitzvah* is absolved from performing another *mitzvah*" (at the same time). On the same page, Rashi explains why people who travel in order to perform a *mitzvah* are absolved from doing another *mitzvah*, even at night when they are resting and ostensibly not engaged in the performance of the said *mitzvah*, because, says Rashi, "They are working and worry (or troubled by–*terudim*) about the *mitzvah* that they have to perform–*mishum sheheim terudim vedoagim bemachshevet hamitzvah*.

4. *Tosefot Sukkah*, ibid., where the *gemara* says that a groom (*chatan*) is absolved from saying the *Shema*, states, "because he cannot concentrate." He is *tarud bemachshavto*. The same is true of the bereaved: He is preoccupied with the dead, with death, and with funeral arrangements. To do a *mitzvah*, one has to have a clear mind. See Rabbi Boon, op. cit.

The entire process of mourning consists of withdrawal from life and of identification with the dead. How then can a person engaged in identification with death engage in the performance of a *mitzvah*, which identifies one with life and brings one nearer to God, the antithesis of death?

offer a warm touch, a kind word, a helpful deed, and to be open-minded, nonjudgmental, understanding, and sympathetic. These are the things that are usually offered, it is hoped, by family and friends. They must be useful momentarily and even in the long run, but they do not answer the deep and profound question, "Why do we suffer and die? Is all our trouble worth it?"

These questions presuppose that our life has purpose and meaning. They assume that, when we complain, there is someone to complain to. The question is, "Do we all agree about that?"

Some thoughtful people believe there is no creation and no Creator. The universe and all therein just happen to exist. They evolve continually. We are merely a passing phase in its development. The world has neither meaning nor purpose. It just is. There is no Law and there is no Law Giver. How can we complain or ask questions about good and evil, life and death, and all the other things we complain about, when there is no one of whom to ask or from whom to receive an answer. In such a world, death and life are meaningless. Pity and compassion are no more virtuous than pain and cruelty are vicious. All we do and work for is really only to advance our own selfish needs of survival, while it lasts. We come and go, in and out from this world, not any differently from a beast of the field or a man-made machine that has run its course and stopped functioning. Life has no goal. Death has no meaning. We come from nothing and return to nothing! That is the sum total of mankind. No questions asked and no answers given. This is the world of the machine. Deux ex machina. No God, no values, no questions!

There are, however, men of thought who maintain that indeed there is a God. Indeed, He created the universe and all in it. There is a Law, but He, the Law Giver, just detached Himself from it. When God created the world and its laws, He left them to be to themselves and He minds His own business. Like a bowler, He merely rolled the ball and then drew Himself away from it. This is by and large the philosophy of deism. It is beautiful. God and mankind mind their own business, as it were. People are responsible for their own affairs. The question, though, which we are entitled to ask under these circumstances, then, is, how can a God, Who is omnipresent, omnipotent, and omniscient, be so cold and immovable when He sees how the world and the creatures therein, which He created, suffer so much and also be so immovable, cold, and unresponsive to their plight? We need not go through a litany of pain and suffering, death and destruction, cruelty to each other, nature's destructive fury, and the evil stalking the land in order to ask the questions, "Why cannot this God respond? Is it just because He created us to be on our own? If so, we might as well have come into the world by accident. If God does not respond to His creatures' needs and He still is omniscient, then He must be heartless, without compassion, pity, or mercy. Such a God is a flawed God. He is lacking in His perfection. He is incapable! He lacks compassion. He cannot show mercy! He cannot respond to our need. Therefore, we cannot turn to Him. Therefore all our questions are meaningless. We might as well be silent, unless, of course, this God is not only heartless but also purposefully cruel. He just minds His own business!

In defining human character types, the rabbis say that there are people "Who say, 'My property is mine and yours is yours.' Such people show an average character, but some say such people show a characteristic of Sodom."[5] We all know that Sodom epitomizes mankind's cruelty to mankind, selfishness, evil, and heartlessness. No one can accept this characteristic as desirable in mankind. Can we accept it as being part of God? Even if we say that it is average for us to say "each man for himself," can we tolerate such a cavalier attitude on the part of God? Surely no and once more no!

Indeed, there are some cynics who maintain that God must be cruel. He is a sadist! How else can He stand by and see how His creatures suffer and not come to their aid? Whether there is ground for such reasoning or not is immaterial. From the point of view of the one who suffers, there is no practical difference between the view that holds that God does not exist and the one that says He does exist but is heartless or cruel, because we, the poor humans, are doomed to an existence that cannot be altered. The basis for asking questions and for complaining is the assumption that reality can be changed. However, if it cannot be changed, what difference does it make whether it is because we live in a mechanical world or a world created by a God Who is either not interested in His creation and shows it no pity or a God Who is interested in it only to the extent that He inflicts pain and sorrow upon it? Those who mourn their lot in life will fare just the same. Their lot will not change. Their life has no intrinsic value,

---

5. *Avot* 5:13.

needs that the stories and words of comfort in this volume are addressed and it is from their content that I would like to express some of
the salient views they take, as well as their philosophical implications
about the nature of life and the purpose of our life and our destiny in
this world.

The very first thing we learn from what the mourners say, and
how the sages have comforted them through the ages, is that they
believe in the existence of God, a God Who created the universe, a God
Who is omniscient, omnipresent, and omnipotent. He is the God Who
not only brought the world and all creatures into existence but Who
also cares for, maintains, and relates to these very creatures as well as all
that is in the world. He is also a God of mercy, compassion, and
kindness. He is a God to Whom we can turn in time of trouble and
sorrow. That is why in time of bereavement we demand to know why
He allows us to suffer, why He allows pain to take place, why parents
lose children and children, parents. Because we know that He is
capable of preventing evil from taking place, we demand to know why
He does not stop all evil.

We also believe that He is a God of justice, Who has endowed us
with the right to choose between good and evil, right and wrong.
Therefore, we demand from God no less. We want Him to live by no
less a standard than the one He set up for mankind. We demand He
should keep His standards. That is why we complain to Him when we
hurt for no good reason.

The second lesson we must derive from the teachings of the rabbis
is that it is all right for people in trouble to cry out in pain. Over and over
again, we learn that those who mourn and complain are not admon-
ished for doing so. On the contrary, their complaints are taken as a
natural human reaction to suffering. It is part of the mourning process
and the state of bereavement. Indeed, the rabbis teach that only those
who are bereaved are allowed to grieve and to weep, because they
mourn the dead. Generally, however, we are prohibited to cry and weep
altogether, because it reflects a lack of faith and unwillingness to accept
our lot in life and whatever God has decreed. To grieve for the dead,
however, is the natural thing to do. It expresses our struggle to survive
and to resist death. It reflects the supremacy of the soul over the body.[9]

---

9. Maharsha. Commentary on *Shabbat* 105b: " 'It is forbidden for people to grieve
and cry because one is allowed to cry only over the dead . . . [not to cry] is considered

When Rabbi Meir lost his two sons, he refused to accept their death until his wife taught him by way of a parable that, like all gifts, his sons had also been a gift and had to be returned. Rabbi Yochanan ben Zakkai refused to be comforted. He, too, could not accept the loss of his son until his disciple Rabbi Eleazar ben Aroch taught him that he should consider himself fortunate to be able to discharge his duties fully. Both Rabbi Meir and Rabbi Yochanan ben Zakkai had questions of God. They had complaints about why their children had died. That is why they refused to be comforted. The most renowned complainer, of course, is Job. Indeed, he complained so much that his friends accused him of being a man of little faith and indeed of being guilty of blasphemy.[10] Yet, at the end of the story, Job is vindicated. God Himself justifies Job's right to complain, if not the nature of his complaints, when He reproves Job's friends for attacking Job. Says He, "My wrath is kindled against you, and against your two friends; for you have not spoken of Me and the things that are right, as my servant Job has."[11] What is it they said, and what was it that Job had said? They tried to vindicate God against Job's demands for justice. They tried to blame Job for his own problems.

Job, on the other hand, blamed God. He demanded to know why he had been punished. He proclaimed his innocence. He blamed God for his trouble. Now God vindicates him. When we are in trouble, when we are in pain, and when we see injustice done and the innocent suffer and we do not know why, we have a right to ask why. We have a duty to demand justice from God. We have reason to begin to doubt. That is what Job did. That is what God said he had a right to do. That is also what Abraham did when he stood up for the people of Sodom. "Shall not the Judge of all the earth do justly?"[12] demanded Abraham of God. That is what every man and woman in mourning cries out to know. That is what all bereaved people express in their time of anguish and sorrow. They cry out, "Why?"

---

by God to be part of the principle of the Fear of Heaven." (In other words, when one cries one shows that one does not accept life as it is (decreed by God) and therefore shows a lack of faith.)

See also *Moed Katan* 27a: "Three days (the first three days of *shiva*) are set aside for crying, seven for eulogizing. . . ."

10. Job 11:14, 15:3–4, and 35, for example, and Baba Batra 16a.
11. Ibid., 42:7.
12. Genesis 18:25.

The thing then, is to say to them, "It's okay. Express your pain. Shout. Complain. Cry. God hears you. You don't have to feel guilty about doing that. You have illustrious examples to follow. They, too, cried. They, too, wanted to know why them. They too had their arguments with God. And God understood them. He knew their pain and suffering. He accepted their cries. He ultimately answered them. Go ahead. Cry if you have to. Ask questions if you have the need to. Be honest; express your thoughts and your feelings. Now, when death is before your eyes, you are facing the moment of truth. You need not pretend. Do not be like Job's friends. Be like Job. If you know what to say, say it. God will hear you. He will heal you and comfort you.

That is what we learn from the words of comfort that have come down to us through the ages.

The third lesson we learn from the nature of the questions the bereaved ask and the answers the sages have given must be the belief in the existence and survival of the soul, the existence of heaven, reward and punishment, and that we are responsible beings, who are accountable for our acts on this earth. All of these are classical ideas. They make up the bedrock of mankind's universal beliefs. When survivors are told that their loved ones are not terminated at the grave but that their souls continue to live, they are comforted. That is not merely a reflexive response brought on by their desire to cling to the life of those whom they love and miss. People are not stupid. They do not live in a land of fantasy. When death strikes their family they do not lose their mind. They hurt but they also continue to think. Therefore, when they find comfort in the words of the sages who tell them that their loved one continues to be in heaven, that the soul of their dear one is alive, it not merely gratifies their emotional needs but also appeals to their mind. They intuitively know that life, which has meaning in and of itself, cannot suddenly be extinguished. It must continue in another form. The soul must live on. Our suffering on earth cannot end in a grand finale at the grave. It must have some compensation. There must be a balance to life and to nature. The wicked cannot simply escape to the grave. They must be brought to account. A balance in life, nature, and the total universe must be maintained. These are the intuitive human feelings, thoughts, and ideals every person has. Death merely brings them up to the surface. In some people, it does so more poignantly, in others, less so, but all go through this process of questioning, feeling, and thinking about life.

Some people may find death too crushing and give up on life altogether. To do that means, if we take the implications of such a decision to their final conclusion, to give up any attempt at justifying any moral order in society and to accept that which gives us the means of making it easier and better for us to live. Such a social order smacks of representing a social placebo, a crutch to lean on, and a society with a real replica of Aldous Huxley's *Brave New World*,[13] in which everybody signs on to die under the most convenient conditions. It reduces life to meaninglessness. It eliminates all substance from all moral questions. It reduces life to a point in time between birth and death. It removes all cause for either joy or sadness. Most people do not accept such a view of life. Most people believe in a life that has meaning, purpose, and continuity. They accept the ideals that expand the faith in a universe that has a Creator Who has created human beings, and they accept that the two interact with one another. They also believe that just as we are responsible for ourselves and the universe, our Creator is also responsible for us and our survival.

At no time do average people express their belief in these ideals more strongly and fervently than when they come face-to-face with the reality of death. At times of bereavement, when we see our most dearly beloved depart this world and we elliptically reflect upon the meaning of our own existence, we affirm our faith in a life after death, the survival of the soul, the existence of God, the need to lead an accountable life, and our interrelationship with God, our Creator. We do this by the questions we ask, by the complaints we utter, by the grief we feel, by the mourning we show, and ultimately by the comfort we accept.

When we read carefully the stories the sages have used to comfort the bereaved and each other through the ages and the parables in which those who mourned have time and again in every generation found comfort, consolation, and peace of mind, we see that all of them carry the same messages, even though the messages may be cloaked in different words. Whether it is the story of Beruriah, Rabbi Meir's wife, who comforted him at the loss of their two sons; whether we see this world as a sandcastle or a vestibule in which we must prepare ourselves in order to be ready to enter the next one; whether or not we see in

---

13. Aldous Huxley, *Brave New World* (New York: Harper & Row, 1946), pp. 237–259.

heaven a topsy-turvy world, whether we ask what kind of person has and what kind does not have a portion in the world to come; or whether we tell the mourner to take a lesson from other human beings in their time of grief, the lessons are always the same: there is a God; there is a soul; the soul survives; only the body dies; there is reward after life; death does not end all.

These messages have been repeated over and over again because they appeal to the basic beliefs of the people who needed to be comforted. They have been retold by the leaders of every generation because they encapsulate the universal faith of mankind, that is, the belief in our transcendent quality, our spiritual dimension, the existence of a soul that survives the body, and our awareness of God! That is why these messages are comforting to mourners. They not only make mourners feel comfortable in the knowledge that they and their dear one will meet again but also express an eternal truth. And the strength and the quality of that truth bring comfort to the bereaved. That truth is God Himself.[14] The rabbis teach us that one of the names by which God is called is *emet* [15] and that His seal is also *emet*.[16] It means truth. It consists of three letters (אמת). These letters are the first, the middle, and the last letters of the Hebrew alphabet. Thus, they conclude, God is there at the beginning, the middle, and the end.[17] He is

---

14. Jeremiah 10:10 – "*Vadoshem Elokim emet hu Elokim chayim umelech olan*" – should be translated "But the Lord is the God of Truth, He is the God of life, and He is the King of eternity."

15. *Midrash Rabbah, Vayikra (Tzav)* 9:9: Said Rabbi Yudan, "Peace is great because the name of God is Peace, for it is written, '. . . And he called the Lord *Shalom*' (Judges 6:24). That is, comments the *Anaf Yosef*, 'Perfection belongs only to God.' "

See also the *Midrash Rabbah* on *Bamidbar* 11:18 – "Great is peace because the name of God – *Makom* – is called Peace."

16. *Shabbat* 55a, *Sanhedrin* 64a, *Yoma* 69b, *Midrash Rabbah*, Genesis 81:2, and *Midrash Rabbah*, Deuteronomy 1:7.

17. Commenting on *Shabbat* 55a, Rashi states, "The middle, the first, and the last letters of the alphabet [are] based on the verse 'I am the first and I am the last and besides me there is no God' (Isaiah 44:6)." Rashi leaves out the clause beginning with "and besides . . ." and instead adds the words "*Va'ani hu* – and I am He," as if to say, "That's it! *Nothing* and *no one else!*"

The difference between saying that God's name is called *emet* and saying that His seal is *emet* is that in the first case, we speak of the essence of God and in the second, of the manifestation of God. Thus we conclude that when it comes to bringing peace there is no difference between God's essence and His manifestation. Peace is immutable. To give people peace is a Divine Act.

there at all times.[18] His truth, we might say, is present when a person is born, when a person lives, and when a person dies. Through our entire existence we cannot escape the truth of the presence of God. When we die, both we and our survivors experience it again. That is why the words that point to the existence of God are really the only true words of comfort. That is why we are comforted by them!

The fourth lesson is that, just as from the words of comfort we learn about our beliefs about ourselves, about God, about the soul, about the body, and about Heaven, we also learn from them what life on this earth is all about. Most of all, we may draw from these stories some lessons about what constitutes success in life and what are the goals we ought to pursue in our earthly and transient life.

The words and the stories that have brought people most of their sought-after comfort direct us to pursue in this world a life of righteousness, piety, humility, kindness, compassion, and understanding toward our fellows. They tell us that a life of scholarship and learning is the most noble pursuit. They measure our success, not by how rich we have become but by how much we have helped others. The purpose of keeping the commandments is to improve the lot of mankind, not oneself. The virtue of the righteous is not that they have merely kept to themselves and did not bother anybody but that they have helped others. They are mourned not because they died but because without their presence their generation is left helpless. Success is not measured by social popularity, political power, or economic wealth but by the human service expressed through one's love, care, concern, support, work, and self-sacrifice on behalf of the spiritual and material well-being of others, consisting of individuals, communities, and countries. People who do these things go to heaven. Such people can expect, merit, and indeed receive a reward in heaven.

The path to paradise goes through the hearts of the people. Mankind's journey in life may have started when we were created as having a soul, but after we came upon this earth, the only possible way to return is by going through the corridors of human needs. That, too, is the purpose of God's commandments. They are to help us to return

---

18. Ibid. *Shabbat* and *Midrash*, Deuteronomy. On the word *"emet"*–"truth"–in *Sanhedrin*, ibid., Rashi comments: "When the king is pleased and agrees with his servants he cosigns with them their decrees with his own seal." Surely God shares in the comforting of all who mourn too!

back to heaven by helping and showing us how to discharge our duties here on earth. With each one of the commandments that we perform, we build another rung onto the ladder that leads from earth back to heaven. That is also the message of the dream Jacob had in Genesis, in which he sees angels of God going up on the ladder.[19] Those angels represented the good deeds people perform going up to heaven to await the soul's return.[20] That is the message of that story. Ever since then, we have tried to climb on such a ladder. All of us build our own ladder, making up our own rungs on it and setting the pace of our climbing by the zeal of our performance of God's commandments. These commandments are encapsulated in one small phrase, "Love your neighbor as yourself."[21] When we have achieved that goal on earth, we are sure to go to heaven in the world to come.

This is the meaning of the stories about the two brothers who gave their lives to save the city, as well as the references to the discharged commandments that are waiting to greet us upon our arrival in heaven, the self-denial of Rabbi Judah the Prince for the sake of others and the call to do loving-kindness, the praise of scholarship, the exultation of giving charity, and the bemoaning of the death of spiritual leaders. Such stories touch the human soul. The survivors know that it is not the amount of riches left behind but the amount shared with others in need, the help extended to other people, the amount of time spent learning, and involvement in the welfare of the public that really count. That is why the bereaved find comfort in the knowledge and the information given them, by those who console them, about the deceased and the deceased's good work in life. When they hear such good things about the departed, they know instinctively not only that their loved one's name will be remembered on earth but also, and more important, that their loved one will be secure in heaven. That is the reason why and the significance of the fact that the mourners are comforted when they hear that life does not stop at the grave and that there is a place in heaven for the soul of their dearly beloved. They know there is an afterlife. When they hear their dear one praised for good work, they also know their dear one will be praised in heaven too. That brings them comfort!

---

19. Genesis 28:12.
20. *Midrash Tanchuma*, Genesis *Vayeitzei* 3.
21. Leviticus 19:8.

The fifth lesson we learn is that the bereaved have a specific concept of life and death. The bereaved regard life in this world as a transient stage in our existence. They consider that the soul and the body have been put together by God, that upon death the soul departs from the body and returns to the world of the spirit, and that the body disintegrates. Death, then, is not a termination of life but a return of the soul to its eternal abode and a return of the body to its natural state – disintegration, change, and earth. Death is thus not a conclusion to life but a point in the migration of the soul between heaven and earth and back again. The bereaved show us also that they believe we are accountable for what we do in this world. That view of life in and of itself is a source of comfort and help to mourners. That in fact they believe in it is expressed in their acceptance of such stories as Rabbi Judah's reply to his friend Antoninus, in which he tells him that in the future God will judge the body and the soul together (it also implies a belief in the resurrection of the dead), and the references to the survival of the soul – that the righteous go to Heaven and that all the souls are brought before God for judgment. The acceptance of such views by those in bereavement and the mere fact that mourners find comfort in them show that mourners have an inner faith in the reality of the ideas that are inherent in those views. If we were not to hold these views, we could never have found them to be a source of comfort and consolation in the time of our greatest need and sorrow!

The sixth lesson is that all people have a sense of responsibility for the welfare and survival of their fellow people. Survivors cannot accept the death of their loved ones because they have a feeling that it was in their power to save them and because they did not, they must be responsible for their death. "If only they had done this or that, if only they had said the right things, taken them to the right physician, or given them the right thing in life, they would not have died." Such are the thoughts that go through the mind of many a parent whose child dies, of a husband whose wife dies, and of children whose parents die, and who are left behind thinking and wondering what it is they could have done that would have saved their dear one, what it was they did that drove the loved one to an earlier death, or what it was that even deprived him or her of a little more happiness in this world. All these feelings explode in a burst of guilt.[22]

---

22. See the chapter "The Comforting of Rabbi Yochanan ben Zakkai" and the notes referring to Robert Jay Lifton.

It is devastating to survivors. It makes their life worse than death, because they constantly live a life of self-torture. They punish themselves for what they perceive to be their responsibility for not having saved their dearly beloved. Such people express their guilt in excessive mourning, refusal to lead a normal life, withdrawal from the outside world, and development of an inward-looking point of view. They wallow in their own self-pity and expect all their friends and relatives to join them.[23] Such a response to bereavement can come only from a heightened, misguided sense of one's own power and ability to affect the lives of others and even to determine their death.

This kind of sense of responsibility may be carried to the extreme by those who do not accept comfort.[24]

They want all life to stop and stand still. They want to make their memories of the past the sum total of their life now. This is impossible. When death strikes, everything changes. Nothing remains the same for anybody. These people, however, expect life to stop with them. They refuse to accept the new reality. They say if they cannot have their loved one on their terms, then they will at least live life on their terms. They assume that they can be in charge of life. When, however, life is wrenched out of their control with the death of the one they love, they begin to feel guilty for allowing it to happen. Their guilt overcomes them. They are riddled with it and they cannot see anything else in life.[25]

There is neither help nor comfort for such people. They see themselves as failures, as inadequate beings, and as having lost control over life. When men lose wives or parents lose children, they also lose control, power, and influence over the person through whom they saw their own life extended, and thus they develop a sense of guilt and inadequacy. Such people knew they had control and now they do not. Those who had been their world are taken from them. Are they not to be blamed for that? Such people will return to normalcy only when they are shown or are jolted into realizing that they are not responsible for what happened either to the dead or to themselves. Only when they realize they have no control over the lives of others and that life and death are in the hands of God can their guilt be removed and

---

23. Such, alas, has been my experience on numerous occasions of encountering the bereaved.

24. See n. 18, op. cit.

25. Ibid.

self-esteem, value, and adequacy as a human being be restored.[26] Only when they realize that being responsible for the welfare of others and giving love and care and direction in life are not the same as having control over life and death do they shed their feeling of guilt. This happens when they realize that while they may be trustees over life, they are not the creators of it, and while they may be borrowers, they are not the owners of life. When this occurs, they recognize that life and death are in the hands of God.[27] Once this takes place, their guilt is removed, they return to life, and they accept our comforting.[28]

This we learn from the story of Rabbi Yochanan ben Zakkai and from the countless number of people in every age who have accepted the comfort of their friends and relatives only after they became aware of the fact that life and death are not in their hands and that they, therefore, should not feel guilty for the death of their dear ones or for their own inadequacies.

People who realize their own limitations also lower their expectations of themselves and others. They are more able to accept the adversities of life. That, too, is a lesson of life we learn from the bereaved.

The seventh lesson is that human beings are finite, that we are limited in what we can do, and that we are mortal, and therefore our comforting of each other is also limited. God alone is eternal and all-powerful and therefore He alone can provide us with the ultimate comfort we need, deserve, and yearn to receive.

When we come to comfort our fellow creatures in their saddest hour we fall back on these ideas and draw on universally held human beliefs in order to console our fellow human beings in trouble and grief. We remind them about the nature of life, the purpose of our existence, the meaning of death, the survival of the soul, and the soul's return to heaven and the presence of its Creator, God. In bringing this to the attention of mourners, we also subtly remind them that all of us are mortal. We all die. We are not God. Our power is limited. Our knowledge is confined to our experience. Our life is merely a passing shadow. And our dear ones are a gift that must be returned. If we are

---

26. Ibid.

27. See the chapter on Rabbi Meir and the death of his sons, "All Gifts Must Be Returned." That too is the moral of the story of Job.

28. See the chapter "The Comforting of Rabbi Yochanan ben Zakkai."

lucky enough to be able to return in peace to Him who entrusted them to us for safekeeping both their soul and their gifts, we should count ourselves fortunate and blessed. That is all we can do. Yes, that is all the survivors can do, and that is all that those who come to comfort us can say! That is why Rabbi Yochanan ben Zakkai, even though he accepted the words of his great disciple Rabbi Eleazar ben Aroch, said to him, "You have comforted me as men can comfort." This is the comfort that man can offer. It is the maximum amount, given the limitations of human beings, that we can do to comfort our fellows, but is it enough?

What Rabbi Yochanan ben Zakkai seems to say is quite simple. Such comfort as that offered by his disciple is the most anyone can give. One should not and therefore cannot expect any more. Given these circumstances, a mourner should accept such words and be comforted. However, in reality they do not remove the pain, the sadness, the sorrow, the heartbreak, or the feelings of isolation, loneliness, helplessness, frustration, and guilt that the bereaved is thrust into at the death of a loved one. The depth of the bereavement of mourners is never fathomed by other people no matter how well-meaning and sympathetic they are or how much empathy they show. Only the bereaved knows what hurts and how much it hurts. Coming from others, however, the words spoken and the ideas expressed are, nevertheless, enough. No one should expect from others more than they can give, but from God, from God, we have reason to expect more. Rabbi Yochanan ben Zakkai thus settled for and indeed accepted the words of comfort offered to him by his disciple, as one man from another only could. However, when he did so, he did so in such a way as to tell us, "From God we expect more." From God, when all is said and done, we may expect the total removal of all suffering. That is why Rabbi Yochanan ben Zakkai said to his disciple, "You have comforted me as anyone can comfort," but not God. God has yet to comfort me! He must and *can* do better![29]

---

29. Ibid. Perhaps therein lies also the clue to the meaning of the discussion between Moses and God in Exodus 33:12–23. Moses' quest to know God was never fulfilled. His death too is an example of the same problem that faced Rabbi Yochanan ben Zakkai, because Moses died in search of the Promised Land, which he never entered. Rabbi Yochanan accepted the painful comforting of people. The comforting of God he never received. In a way, that too was a form of death. He stopped his intellectual struggle with God, though he remained a life. Moses carried his quest to his last breath. Both men were left without an answer to their question, because mankind cannot

The troubling question is not really one about comforting but about the removal of all suffering altogether. The question is expressed in a somewhat different context in the Talmud. We are told that Rabbi Meir was once greatly bothered by a band of ruffians who had moved into his area. They annoyed him to the limits of his endurance, until he finally began to pray for their death. When his wife, Beruriah, heard him, she turned to him and said, "You must be thinking that one is allowed to pray for the death of the wicked because it is written, 'Let *chata'im* cease' [that is, the Hebrew word *chata'im*, which means sin, can also be read as *chotim*—sinner, and therefore it could mean either sin or

---

fathom that answer. We can see only God's footprints in history, never His countenance. We can strive to come as close to God as possible but can never come into the inner mystery of God!

The *Midrash Rabbah Hamevuar* on Deuteronomy, *Vezot Haberachah* 11:8, states, "When the time came for Moses to depart from this world, the Holy One, blessed be He, said to him, 'Your days have arrived' (Deuteronomy 31:14). Moses then said to God, 'Master of the Universe, after all this trouble (which I went through), you tell me, "Your days have arrived!" I shall not die, on the contrary, I shall live and tell of the works of the Lord' (Psalms 118:17). God then said to Moses 'You cannot do that because that is the whole man' (Ecclesiastes 12:13)." In other words, the essence of being human is that we must die.

The question arises, What is the difference between the comfort that comes from other people and the comfort that comes from God?

The *Yalkut Shimoni Cheilek Sheimi* on the *Nevi'im Rishonim Va'acharonim*. (Jerusalem, 1959), p. 791, sect. 445, on the verse *"yomar Elokeichem*—Saith your God" brings the following statement:

> Rabbi Chaninah bar Papah and Rabbi Shimon. Rabbi Chaninah bar Papah said:
> Israel said to Isaiah, "Isaiah our Teacher, can you say that you not come to comfort only the generation in whose time the Temple was destroyed?" He said to them, "I have come to comfort all the generations, for it is not written, "Said your God," but instead it is written, "Your God will say."

And on page 800, section 474, on the verse "I, only I, am the one who comforts you," (Isaiah 51:12) we read:

> Said Rabbi Shimon ben Gamliel, "It is the nature of a father to comfort in the manner in which a father comforts and it is the nature of a mother to comfort in the manner in which a mother comforts. Therefore God said, "I will comfort you both as a father and as a mother"; thus it is written, "I, only I [the word "I" is repeated], am the one who comforts you."

We can deduce from these two passages in the *Yalkut* that whereas comforting by people is temporary and only a halfway measure, such as that of the father or the mother, God's comforting is permanent and complete. It is perfect, as God Himself is perfect. That is why it must be left for the end of days, when each of us, too, reaches a state of perfection, namely, no death.

sinners], and you, Rabbi Meir, take it to mean sinners, but it is really written *chata'im*, which means sin! Furthermore, if you look at the conclusion of the verse, you will see that it says, 'And let the wicked men be no more.' Thus the whole verse should read, 'When sin will cease, the wicked men will be no more.' Therefore," Beruriah concluded, "you should rather pray that they should repent and then there will be no more wickedness." He did pray for them, the story concludes, "and they repented."[30]

The important point that Beruriah makes to her husband is that the trouble with the world consists not in the existence of wicked people but in the existence of wickedness. Remove wickedness and remove sin and there will be no wicked people and no sinners. The problem with the bereaved is not only that they suffer but that suffering exists. Their tragic loss, though very personal and deeply private, also raises with them the great public and general question of the existence of death. They ask also, "Why is there suffering?" For that question there is no comfort. That is why Rabbi Yochanan ben Zakkai said, "You have comforted me as anyone can." People can assuage individual pain. They cannot, however, explain or remove universal pain. Weltschmerz, the pain of the world, remains unexplained. Rabbi Yochanan ben Zakkai was astute enough to perceive it, honest enough to say it, and courageous enough to demand, if only by implication, an answer.

Indeed, the quest for the removal of death has been institutionalized in the Jewish funeral ritual. At the conclusion of the funeral service at the cemetery, the following prayer is said, "He will destroy death forever; the Lord God will wipe away tears from all faces . . . for the Lord has spoken it."

That is the ultimate way of comforting the mourners and the final wish for mankind's triumph over death, which will come as the final realization of God's promise and the removal of all evil from the world. But until that time comes, man can only find comfort in one another's sympathy![31]

When the Jewish people witnessed the destruction of the Temple and experienced their exile, they lost all hope and fell into a state of

---

30. *Berachot* 10a. See also the chapter "All Gifts Must Be Returned."

31. *Yoreh Dei'ah*, op. cit., 376:4, especially the commentary by Beth Lechem Yehudah.

despair. They refused to be comforted. The *Midrash* relates that God sent them the prophets to comfort and console them and promise them future redemption.

However, they refused to be comforted. They could not accept the comfort of mere mortals. Finally, the *Midrash* continues, God sent them the prophet Isaiah, who said to them, "Comfort ye, comfort ye, my people, saith the Lord your God," which means that Isaiah, God's messenger, says to the Jews, "God says [not "I say"], 'Comfort ye, comfort ye, my people.' " When the Jewish people heard that God Himself was comforting them, they were comforted.[32]

Ultimately, after all is said and done, and all of us have exhausted ourselves both physically and mentally to comfort our bereaved relative, friend, neighbor and fellow human being, there comes a point when we can do no more. Just as human beings are limited in physical, intellectual, spiritual, and emotional power by virtue of their being human, so are they limited in their ability to bring comfort to each other. Just as we cannot control life or death, we cannot give absolute

---

32. Isaiah 40:1.

Midrash Rabbah Hamevuar, Genesis 100:9, infers from a minor to a major premise (*kal vechomer*) that God's comforting of the Jewish people in the days of the Messiah will be absolute by comparing it to the comforting of Joseph's brothers by Joseph:

> Joseph, who spoke softly with his brothers, was able to comfort them (even though he used the word "comfort"—*vayinachem*—only once (Genesis 50:2). God, Who used the same word twice, will surely comfort them (for good) when He will come to comfort Jerusalem. Therefore it is written *nachamu, nachamu ami*—"comfort ye, comfort ye, my people," for you will be comforted by God in the absolute sense.

See also the Commentary of the *Midrash Rabbah Hamevuar*, Genesis vol. 4, p. 363.

See also ibid., p. 368: For the refusal of the children of Israel to be comforted by all the prophets and the Patriarchs, and, finally, reluctantly accepting comfort only at the hands of God, see *Yalkut Shimoni Cheilek Sheini, Nevi'im Rishonim Va'acharonim.* (Jerusalem, 1959), pp. 790–791.

After enumerating all the prophets, including the Patriarchs, whose comforting words were rejected by the Jews, the *Yalkut* section 443 on Isaiah 40:1 says:

> All of them immediately went to God and said to Him, "Master of the universe, she (the *Knesset Yisrael*) does not accept comfort from us." Thus it is written, "The poor one who is tossed about by the storm is not comforted" (Isaiah 54:11). God then said to them, "I and you shall go together and comfort her." If so, it should not have been written, "Comfort ye, comfort ye, my people," but rather, "They have comforted, they have comforted my people." Therefore, it means that God said, "It is only proper that I alone and no one else should go to comfort her." That's why it is written, "Comfort ye, comfort ye, my people . . ."

See also *Midrash Rabbah*, Leviticus 10:2, Genesis 100:13, the *Shitah Chadasha Lebirkat Ya'akov* 3 (p. 396, ibid.), and *Ayacha* 1:23.

comfort to each other. That, too, is part of our human condition, for to bring absolute comfort to each other means to remove the very tragic nature of human existence.[33] If we were able to absolutely assuage one another's suffering, we would also be able to remove from each other death itself and thus soar to the heights of an angel and be God-like. Unfortunately, God has made us a little lower than the angels. That applies to all areas of human experience. When faced with the tragedy of death and the ultimate question of why we suffer, we can bring comfort to each other and answer the question "only as anyone can." That may not be a good enough answer, unfortunately, the same as when it was not good enough for Rabbi Yochanan ben Zakkai or for the Jewish people when the Temple was destroyed. Only when the answer comes from Him Who is the Giver of life and death, pleasure and pain, and happiness and suffering will we truly be comforted. May that time come when all who suffer in loneliness, all who carry on their shoulders the pain of the world, and all those who toil under the burdens of the entire suffering of humanity hear the proclamation from God Himself, "Comfort ye, comfort ye, my people" and be fully comforted, for then they shall be comforted only as God can comfort!

---

33. The tragic sense of life is that we know we are going to die and can do nothing about it. Comforting the bereaved is to diminish the tragedy of life.

Bibliography

Avot Derabbi Natan (at the end of) *Talmud Bavli Avodah Zarah*. Vilna: The Widow and Brothers Romm, 1921.

Azkari, Elazar Rabbi. *Peirush: Ba'al Sefer Chareidim* on *Berachot, Talmud Yerushalmi*. Jerusalem: Machon Chatam Sofer, 1970.

Caspi, Rabbi Yosef. *Even Caspi on Lamentations*. Vienna, 1853.

de Unamuno, Miguel. *Tragic Sense of Life*, trans. J. E. Crawford Flitch. NY: Dover, 1954.

Edels, Shmuel Eliezer ben Yehuda Ha-levi (Maharsha). *Chidushei Halachot Va'agadot*.

Epictetus. *Discourses, Book 1*. Great Books of the Western World, vol. 12, trans. George Long. Chicago: Encyclopedia Britannica, 1952.

Frankel, Rabbi David. Commentary on *Berachot* and *Ketubot, Talmud Yerushalmi*. Jerusalem: Machon Chatam Sofer, 1970.

Franklin, Benjamin. *His Life as He Wrote It*, ed. Esmond Wright. Cambridge, MA: Harvard University Press, 1989.

Freud, Sigmund. *Civilization and Its Discontents*. Great Books of the Western World, vol. 54. Chicago: Encyclopedia Britannica, 1952.

Freud, Sigmund. *New Introductory Lectures on Psychoanalysis*. New York: W. W. Norton, 1933.

Gershom bar Yehudah Meor Hagolah. Commentary on *Baba Batra, Talmud Bavli*. Vilna: The Widow and Brothers Romm, 1921.

Graetz, H. *History of the Jews*, vol. II. Philadelphia: Jewish Publication Society, 1891.

Greenwald, Yetuthiel Yehudah. *Kol Bo Al Aveilut*, vol. I. New York: Philipp Feldheim, 1956.

Haga'oth Maimoni'yoth. (Commentary on) *Hilchot Eivel, Mishnch Torah*. Vilna: Avraham Tzi Rosenkrantz and Menachem Mendel Schriftsetzer, 1899.

Hanoch Zundl. *Anaf Yosef* and *Etz Yosef*. Commentaries on *Midrash Rabbah*, vols. I and II. Vilna: The Widow and Brothers Romm, 1896.

High Holy Day Prayer Book. Trans. Philip Birnbaum. New York: Hebrew Publishing, 1951.

Huxley, Aldous. *Brave New World.* New York: Harper & Row, 1946.

Isserles, Moshe (Ramoh). *Mapah Perusah Hagahot Vechidushei Dinim* on the *Shulchan Aruch, Orach Chayim,* vols. I and II, and *Yoreh Dei'ah,* vol. III. New York: *Otzar Halacha,* 1969.

Jourda, José Huertos. *The Existentialism of Miguel de Unamuno.* University of Florida Monographs, Humanities No. 13. Gainesville, FL: University of Florida, 1963.

Karo, Yoseph. *Shulchan Aruch.* New York: *Otzar Halacha,* 1969. *Orach Chayim Sefer M'ginay Eretz* I and II, *Yoreh Dei'ah.*

Kimchi, David ben Yosef ben Kimchi Hasefaradi (Radak). Commentary on Isaiah, *Mikraot Gedolot.* New York: *Hotza'at Pardes,* 1951.

Levin, Yehudah Leib. *Chasidim Mesaprim.* Vol. I. Jerusalem: *Mosad Hari'm Levin,* 1968.

Lifton, Robert Jay. *The Broken Connection.* New York: Simon & Schuster, 1979.

Lifton, Robert Jay. *Death in Life – Survivors of Hiroshima.* New York: Random House, 1967.

Lifton, Robert Jay. *History and Human Survival.* New York: Random House, 1970.

Malbim, Rabbi Meir Leibush. Commentary on the *Tanach* (the Holy Scriptures). Printed in Israel, n.d.

Marcus Aurelius. *Meditations.* Great Books of the Western World, vol. 12, trans. George Long. Chicago: Encyclopedia Britannica, 1952.

Margalit, Rabbi Moshe Peiyrish. *Penei Moshe* and *Tosefot* on *Berachot, Talmud Yerushalmi.* Jerusalem: *Machon Chatam Sofer,* 1970.

Margolis, Max L., and Marx, Alexander. *A History of the Jewish People.* Philadelphia: Jewish Publication Society, 1947.

Matnot Kehunah. Commentary on *Midrash Rabbah,* vols. I and II. Vilna: The Widow and Brothers Romm, 1896.

Menachem Mendel of Kotzk. *Emet Ve'emunah – Divrei Torah Merabeinu Hakadosh.* Tel Aviv: Brodi and Katz, 1971.

Michilta Derabbi Yishmael. With annotations and text corrections by Chaim Shaul Horovitch, ed. Israel Avraham Rabin. 2nd ed. Jerusalem: Vahrman, 1970.

Midrash Mishlei. Vilna: The Widow and the Brothers Romm, 1892. Reprinted, Jerusalem, 1964, ed. Shlomoh Baber.

Midrash Rabbah, vols. I and II. On *Bereishit* (Genesis), *Vayikra* (Leviticus), *Bamidbar* (Numbers), *Devarim* (Deuteronomy), and *Kohelet* (Ecclesiastes). Vilna: The Widow and Brothers Romm, 1896.

Midrash Rabbah Hamevuar. On *Bereishit* (Genesis), vols. I, II, III, and IV; *Shemot* (Exodus), vols. I and II; *Vayikra* (Leviticus), vol. I; *Devarim* (Deuteronomy); Eichah (Lamentations), and Ruth. Jerusalem: *Machon Hamidrash Hamevuar,* 1984–1991.

Midrash Tanchuma. On *Bereishit* (Genesis), *Shemot* (Exodus), *Vayikra* (Leviticus), and *Devarim* (Deuteronomy). Jerusalem: Levin, Epstein, 1962.

Midrash Tehilim Hamechuneh Shachar Tov, with an introduction by Shlomo Baber. Vilna: The Widow and Brothers Romm, 1891. Photographed and reprinted by Vagshal, Jerusalem, 1977.

Mikraot Gedolot. New York: *Hotza'at Pardes,* 1951.

Moshe ben Maimon (Rambam). *Mishneh Torah (Hayad Hachazakah),* 5 vols. Vilna: Avraham Tzvi Rozenkrantz and Reb M. M. Schriftsetzer, 1900.

Nachman of Breslav. *Chayei Maharan.* Jerusalem: *Agudat Meshech Hanachal,* 1984.

_____ . *Sichot Haran.* Jerusalem: *Agudat Meshech Hanachal,* 1985.

_____ . *Yemei Moharnat.* Jerusalem: *Agudat Meshech Hanachal,* 1981.

Naftal, Avraham Moshe. *Hatalmud Veyotzrav,* vol. I, *Dorot Hatanayim.* Tel Aviv: Yehoshua Orenstein, Yavneh Publishing, 1976.

Niederland, William G. "The Problems of the Survivor: Part I–Some Remarks on the
Psychiatric Evaluation of Emotional Disorders in Survivors of Nazi Persecution."
Journal of the Hillside Hospital 10 (1961).

Nisim Gerondi (Rabeinu Nisim-Ran). Commentary on *Nedarim* (Babylonian Talmud).
Vilna: The Widow and Brothers Romm, 1921.

Oppenheim, Avraham. *Eishel Avraham* on *Shulchan Aruch, Orach Chayim,* vol. I., 1959.

Pawelczynska, Anna. *Values and Violence in Auschwitz–a Sociological Analysis.* Trans.
Catherine S. Leach. Berkeley, CA: University of California Press, 1979.

(The) *Pentateuch.* Trans. and explained by Samson Raphael Hirsch. Rendered into
English by Isaac Levy. 2nd ed. London: L. Honig & Sons, 1960.

(The) *Pentateuch and Haftarahs.* Ed. Dr. J. H. Hertz. 2nd ed. London: Soncino Press, 1981.

Peretz, Yehuda Leib. *Yehuda Leib Peretz.* Ed. A. S. Rappoport. Freeport, NY: Books for
Library Press, 1971.

Peretz, Y. L. *Shriften, Naye Fergreserte Oiflage. Zveiter Band.* New York: Hebrew Publishing
Co.

Pesikta Rabbati. Warsaw: Menachem Mendel Yustman, 1892.

Pinto, Yoshiahu ben Yosef (Harif). *Meor Einayim.* Commentary on *Shabbat* in *Ein
Ya'akov.* New York: *Hotza'at Safra,* 1944.

Pirkei Derabbi Eliezer, with Commentary by Rabbi David Luria (Radal). Warsaw: Rabbi
Yaakov Bamberg, 1851.

Sarai, Shmuel. *Tekufat Hamishnah Vehatalmud.* In *Toldot Am Ysrael Biymei Kedem,* vol. I. ed.
H. H. ben-Sasson. Tel Aviv: Devir, 1969.

Sellars, Wilfrid. "Realism and the New Way of Words in Readings," in *Philosophical
Analysis,* selected and edited by Herbert Feigel and Wilfrid Sellars. New York:
Appleton-Century-Crofts, 1949.

Shabetai ben Meir Hakohen (Shach). Commentary on *Shulchan Aruch, Yoreh Dei'ah*

Shitah Chadasha Lebirkat Ya'akov. In *Midrash Rabbah, Hamevuar Bereishit,* vol IV. Jerusalem: *Machon Hamidrash Hamevuar,* 1984.

Shlomo Yitzchaki (Rashi). Commentary on *Tanach, Mikraot Gedolot.* New York:
Hotza'at Pardes, 1951. And *Talmud Bavli.* Vilna: The Widow and Brothers Romm,
1921.

Shmuel Hanagid. *Mavo Hatalmud, Berachot, Talmud Bavli.* Vilna: The Widow and
Brothers Romm, 1895.

Talmud Bavli. On *Avodah Zarah, Avot, Avot Derabbi Natan, Baba Kama, Baba Metzia,
Berachot, Eruvin, Gittin, Kalah Rabbati,, Ketubot, Kiddushin, Megillah, Mishnah Shevi'ith,
Moed Katan, Nidah, Pesachim, Sanhedrin, Semachot, Shabbat, Sotah, Sukkah, Ta'anit,
Yevamot, and Yoma.* Vilna: The Widow and Brothers Romm, 1921.

Talmud Yerushalmi. On *Berachot* and *Ketubot.* Jerusalem: *Machon Chatan Sofer,* 1970.

Tanach: A New Translation of The Holy Scriptures according to the Traditional Hebrew Text.
Philadelphia: Jewish Publication Society, 1985.

Tanach: The Holy Scriptures. Philadelphia: Jewish Publication Society, 1955. And *Torah*

Nevi'im Ketuvim. On the Torah: Genesis, Exodus, Leviticus, Numbers, and Deuteronomy. On The Prophets: Judges, II Samuel, I Kings, Isaiah, Jeremiah, Ezekiel, and Zechariah. On The Writings: Psalms, Proverbs, Job, Ruth, Lamentations, Ecclesiastes, and I Chronicles. Jerusalem: Koren, n. d.

Tolstoy, Leo. "How Much Land Does a Man Need." In Leo Tolstoy, *Stories and Legends*, trans. Dorothy Canfield Fischer. New York: Pantheon Books, n. d.

Torah Nevi'im Ketuvim. Jerusalem: *Hotza'at Koren*, n. d.

Tosefot. Commentary on *Ketubot* (Babylonian Talmud). Vilna: The Widow and Brothers Romm, 1921.

Tuchachinsky, Rabbi Yechiel Michel. *Sefer Gesher Hachayim.* Vols. I, II, and III. 2nd ed. Jerusalem: Nissan Aaaron Tuchachinsky, 1960.

Weisman, Avery, and Hackett, Thomas. "Predilections to Death: Death and Dying as a Psychiatric Problem." *Psychosomatic Medicine* 23 (1961): 232–56.

(Sefer) Yalkut Hamchiri Al Mishlei. Ed. Elazar Halevi. Jerusalem: Grünhoot, 1891.

Yalkut Shimoni. Midrash Al Torah, Nevi'im Uketuvim. Parts one and two. Jerusalem, 1959.

Yehoshua ben Yitzchak (Folk). *Binyan Yehoshua.* Commentary on *Avot Derabbi Natan.* Part of *Avodah Zarah.* Vilna: The Widow and Brothers Romm, 1921.

Zaretzky, David. "The Sand Castle." *Yeted Ne'eman* (6 *Kislev* 5751/23 November, 1991): 6.

Zohar, Sefer Vayikra. Vilna: The Widow and Brothers Romm, 5655.

Index

About the Author

Chaim Rozwaski is the rabbi of the Suburban Park Jewish Center, Congregation Lev Torah in East Meadow, New York. He received ordination from the Hebrew Theological College in 1962 and has served as the spiritual leader of congregations in this country and in England. Born in Poland, Rabbi Rozwaski survived the Holocaust by hiding, as a child, with an aunt, uncle, and partisans in the forest. He has been very active in Jewish organizations, particularly in the areas of the Holocaust, the United Jewish Appeal, and Israel Bonds. His work has garnered him such recognition as being invited to the White House by President Jimmy Carter for the signing of the Camp David peace accord, and for the establishment of the Holocaust Memorial Center. Twice he delivered the opening prayer at the United States House of Representatives. The recipient of a doctorate in Talmudic Law from the Ner Israel Rabbinical College in Baltimore, Maryland, and a master of science in philosophy and education from Purdue University in Indiana, Rabbi Rozwaski has published articles in many magazines, including *Commentary*, *The Jewish Spectator*, and *Midstream*.